MONUMENTAL HUG

DIVORCE, CANCER, GRACE & HEALING

ED MELICK

Monumental Hug: Divorce, Cancer, Grace & Healing

Published by Grace Machines LLC

Footnotes are included on the page where they are cited for ease of reference.

Some names have been changed to protect the privacy of individuals.

First Edition
ISBN: 978-1-7331282-1-6 (softcover)

Cover Design by Ed Melick.
Cover photo by Shannon Melick.

Table of Contents

Introduction 1
1 | The Diagnosis 3
2 | Three Days in May 7
3 | Too Much Information 17
4 | Sweet Diane 21
5 | A Grim Prognosis 29
6 | Insidious Decline 37
7 | Turning a Corner 43
8 | Growing Grace 57
9 | Big Cancer 77
10 | Strands of Grace 89
11 | Non-Standard Care 101
12 | Spreading Grace 113
13 | Healing in the Bible 121
14 | Breaking Bad in Herndon 131
15 | Culminating Grace 143
16 | Insights 153
17 | Healing Grace 163
18 | The Gospel of Grace 169
19 | Monumental Hug 181
Appendix A | The Toll of Cancer 183
Appendix B | If You're Diagnosed with Cancer 187

Introduction

"I love you and I'm proud of you." I couldn't believe these words were coming out of my mouth, given the circumstances. My wife of over 22 years (actually, her lawyer) had destroyed me the day before in court during an initial divorce proceeding, and she had just moved our 13-year-old daughter and half of our belongings into her new apartment. Strangely enough, I was standing with her in her new apartment's bedroom, just after the movers had left, when I uttered these words. They certainly aren't the words you typically hear in divorce situations. What happened the next day—Mother's Day 2008—was far more unusual, sparking a remarkable ten-year journey during which I would discover the realness, power, practicality, and beauty of God's grace.

1 | The Diagnosis

The phone rang on a Thursday evening in late July 2016. It was my ex-wife, Diane, and she sounded worried. She'd left me a voice mail earlier that week expressing concern over something her doctor just found in her blood. She mentioned high levels of bilirubin and I thought, *What's a bilirubin*? She said she was scheduled for an ultrasound the following day and would have better insight into what was going on then. She was clearly concerned that it might be something serious. The next evening, she called again. The ultrasound had identified a growth in her pancreas, which her doctor thought was blocking the release of bile from her liver. They were concerned it was pancreatic cancer. She was scheduled to have a computerized tomography (CT) scan the following Monday to confirm what the ultrasound had shown. Her dad died of pancreatic cancer at age 60 and Diane was currently 56. Things did not look good.

That night as I lay in bed, the seriousness of her situation really sank in. I had a rough night sleeping, alternating between crying, boldly praying for Diane, and fretting about the logistical difficulties of caring for her while living and working a half-hour drive apart. I was heartbroken over what she was facing. Most people understand how deadly pancreatic cancer is and know someone who has faced down the disease. Now it was attacking one of the two people I loved most in the world.

I drove Diane to her CT scan the following Monday and afterward chatted briefly with the radiologist. He said the results were not good, although he was hesitant to provide a lot of detail before generating his full report.

The following Thursday, just one week after receiving that concerned phone call from Diane, we had our first meeting with an oncologist. Two things stood out. First, the doctor felt that Diane was probably inoperable, and that her care would "almost certainly" be palliative. In other words, there was no way to cure the cancer, and the goals were to extend Diane's life and make her as comfortable as possible.

The second thing was the sense of urgency the doctor expressed. He wanted to schedule a stent procedure and biopsy as soon as possible and begin chemotherapy once Diane's bilirubin reached an acceptable level. I would soon learn that this sort of pressure to move fast was common with oncologists—in some cases justifiably so and in some cases, not. Pancreatic cancer is an aggressive form of cancer, and the doctor's assertiveness was not lost on Diane. She wanted to get moving, too. As the doctor walked us down a hallway to the office exit, Diane turned to him and smiled, shook her finger and said, "I'm going to beat this thing and make you famous." All I could think was, *Wouldn't it be cool to beat this thing and make God famous?*

I took Diane to a great restaurant near the doctor's office where she polished off a rack of ribs. She certainly wasn't lacking an appetite! When we went outside and I saw her in the late-afternoon sunlight, her skin looked golden and her eyes were yellow. She joked that she looked like one of Willy Wonka's Oompa Loompas. That was funny, true, and scary all at the same time. I wanted to pray with her, but she said she didn't want to cry, so I hugged her, sneaking in a quick prayer anyway, and said goodbye.

Within two weeks of Diane's call, she had undergone a stent placement procedure and biopsy, and our worst-case suspicions were confirmed. She had adenocarcinoma, the most common (95 percent of cases) and deadly form of pancreatic cancer. The statistics for this type of cancer are frightening. Several sources put the five-year survival rate at 7 percent, when considering all stages. It has been routinely listed as the second worst survival rate of all cancers.[1] Only 15 percent of patients are operable at the time of diagnosis,

---

[1] *Cancer Facts and Figures, 2015*, American Cancer Society. Also, the 8/9/16 version of https://en.wikipedia.org/wiki/List_of_cancer_mortality_rates_in_the_United_States.

and we were told that no one is ever "cured" when surgery is not part of the treatment protocol. The statistics shocked me. I thought, *Haven't we spent hundreds of billions of dollars on cancer research since President Nixon declared war on cancer back in 1971? If so, what good did that money do?*

We were both doing a lot of research into treatment options—or at least we were trying to. We didn't find many "Western medicine" options because, frankly, there aren't many. There is basically some combination of surgery, chemo, and radiation, with only two forms of chemo treatment available for pancreatic cancer. That's it. And they all have abysmal survival statistics associated with them. There seemed to be many more treatment options in the "alternative medicine" camp, but besides the one or two anecdotal success stories that accompanied each one, we couldn't find any supporting data.

I read online that there was data to support various claims, but I couldn't find it. Some alternative medicine stories raved about the existence of such data and how the discoverer wanted to share it freely with everyone, but I couldn't find data on the Web. I kept thinking, *If you want to share it so badly, then post it on the Web already.*

I watched lots of videos, read tons of articles, researched, ordered and read books, and talked to as many people as I could. One thing that stood out was the six-hour PBS documentary *Cancer: The Emperor of All Maladies*, based on the Pulitzer Prize-winning book by Siddhartha Mukherjee. Several things about the film struck me. One was the ugly cycle that has repeated too many times over the years in the treatment of cancer. It goes like this: First, a brutal treatment is developed, like radical mastectomy for breast cancer. Second, it becomes widely accepted and many, many people suffer its effects. Third, someone comes along and questions the approach and gets crucified by the medical establishment. Fourth, people slowly come around and acknowledge the approach is too harsh and ineffective. Finally, a new brutal approach is developed and the cycle repeats. Am I saying that all treatments are like this? No, but way too many are.

I was also struck by the monumental suffering people experienced getting treatment from Western doctors and the difficulty they have getting alternative treatments, often having to flee to other countries. This all seemed ridiculous and pitiful to me, especially in a country that prides itself on having the best healthcare system in the world.

Diane and I quickly fell into two separate camps—me pushing for alternative care and her betting on Western medicine. Diane and I had some difficult conversations about her course of treatment. Given the poor survival rates being quoted to us, I felt she should try an alternative approach to chemotherapy—one that would strengthen her immune system and allow her to avoid the side effects of chemo. She didn't agree and was, at times, quite adamant in her rejection of alternative treatments. On one occasion when I mentioned alternative care, she said something to the effect of, "No f****** way am I going to do that!" Her visceral reaction made me realize a few things. First, she, not I, was facing something very scary, and I couldn't even begin to imagine what it was like. Second, her life decisions were hers to control, not mine. My job ultimately was to extend grace to her no matter what decision she made, and to share opinions as unemotionally and respectfully as possible. Third, her trust was in Western medicine.

In the end, she chose to follow the advice of her oncologist and a surgeon we met from The Johns Hopkins Hospital in Baltimore, Maryland, and begin an extremely toxic regimen of chemo known as Folfirinox. At one point, Diane told the surgeon that his hospital had failed her dad over thirty years ago, but that she was going to give them a second chance. I remember thinking, *Here we go.*

2 | Three Days in May

> God sometimes takes us to places we would never go on our own in order to bring about change that can only happen in those places. This is the redemptive violence of his grace.
>
> Paul Tripp
> Author, Speaker and Pastor

Eight years before Diane's diagnosis, when she and I were still married, I went to my first church men's retreat at the age of forty-six. Up to that point, I couldn't be bothered with such things. I didn't want to waste the time, share a room with someone, or spend the money. Even worse, I was self-righteous and didn't think I needed to go.

That began to change shortly after I arrived and the organizers showed a video entitled *Flame*.[2] In it, the narrator describes three different Hebrew words translated into the English word *love* in the Song of Solomon, a collection of Hebrew love poems in the Bible. One of the words, *raya*, means "friend, companion or soulmate." A second word, *ahava*, represents such a deep affection for, desire to be with, and commitment to someone that your heart aches if you're not together. The third word, *dod*, represents passion and sexual intimacy. The narrator talked about how these three things (i.e., flames) were meant to exist (burn) together and the satisfaction (heat) that results when they do.

Now, here's the awful part. I remember thinking, *I don't have that anymore toward Diane,* for *each* of the words he described. I actually got up, left the meeting room, and went to a private place

---

[2] *Flame* video by Rob Bell. See https://www.youtube.com/watch?v=KYfCXsSmZ7s.

to cry. In that moment I realized how broken my twenty-two-year marriage had become.

I spent the next two days thinking deeply about what had happened, seeking advice from other men at the retreat, and building up the resolve to change. I drove home and immediately hugged my wife. It was something we almost never did in those days. Her response was chilly. She stood with her arms crossed and forehead furrowed when I wrapped my arms around her. I asked her what was wrong, and she said, "You're only hugging me because you went to a men's retreat."

I responded by saying, "That's a good thing, isn't it?" She was unmoved and didn't hug me back.

The next morning, I created a short list of things I was determined to pray about every day. First, I began asking God to profoundly change me—to change the way I think, behave, speak, see, hear, feel, and react. Second, I asked Him to give me uncommon faith, Godly love, and the wisdom of Jesus Christ. Finally, I asked Him to give me five things in my marriage, none of which I had at the time. The following is what I wrote in my prayer notes:

- Change our hearts. Put the strong desire to change in both of us, the ability to do so, and lead us to actually do it.
- I know your will in general. I don't know how we can follow through on it in a practical way after repeatedly hurting each other. What's the answer? Longsuffering? Grace? But how?
- Help us treat each other "as we should."
- Help us have fun together.
- Bring us out of this period with a better marriage than ever—one with Jesus at the core—deeply changed for the better and able to help many others.

I also began striving to treat Diane with more kindness and patience, but it soon became evident that her hurt was deep as she responded with cynicism, indifference, and hostility. I reacted poorly to this and we quickly fell back onto our toxic patterns of behavior.

Eight months later, on a spring morning, I was driving home following a workout at the gym. I had just wrapped up a difficult ten-month consulting assignment six days earlier and was looking forward to exercising more frequently and generally recharging. I was also planning to launch a new business and had lined up some financing from a local bank.

I got a call from my stockbroker who started our conversation by asking me where I was. When I told him I was driving, he asked me to pull over. Once I stopped the car, he told me that my wife had called his office and had them freeze all of our accounts because we were getting divorced. This was news to me. I felt shock and disbelief. It seems that, despite my retreat revelation, I had been in a state of denial. While I knew we had our problems and had admittedly grown apart, we weren't dealing with issues like extramarital affairs, drug use, physical abuse, or bankruptcy. Because of this, I had deluded myself into believing things would never reach the point of separation and divorce.

I sped home, saw Diane's car, and burst into the house in search of her. She was upstairs gathering her things for work. I called out to her from the foyer on the main level and demanded to know why our broker had called me and said what he did. I watched as she moved between rooms across the upstairs landing, repeatedly disappearing and hardly saying a word. After more yelling on my part, she came down the stairs, calmly handed me her lawyer's card, and told me to call her. Then she left for work. She had been well coached. I was stunned.

At that point things got real, fast. As I worked through the initial shock of the following few days, I had several major revelations. The biggest one was that I had slowly come to live in a state of perpetual "un-grace" in my marriage. I had become angry, selfish, impatient, grumpy, and, sometimes, downright mean. I had tried to get my wife to do the things that were important to me by increasingly showing my displeasure with her. I had kept a record of her wrongs, often grumbling and cursing with displeasure, and could barely offer up a smile when I was around her. Of course, she wasn't perfect either, but I realized that the only person I could change was me. I also realized that behaving ungracefully had brought me right to the brink of divorce.

I began to think seriously about the example Jesus Christ set as recorded in the Bible. What I saw was truly amazing. I saw how badly Christ was treated throughout His life by many people He met, and how He was eventually beaten and crucified. I realized that He accepted all of this without lashing out or using His power to force people to change. Instead, He traveled around the countryside teaching and healing the sick, taking the time to listen to the lowliest of people, and even crying with compassion when He saw suffering. This made me realize how badly I had been behaving. Instead of appreciating my wife's differences and using them to help me change and mature, I was continually exerting pressure on her to change.

So, I decided to do several things. I committed to start seeing my wife through God's graceful, loving eyes and not my own selfish ones. I also committed to treating her with grace, no matter what happened. I simply did not want to get into the "tit for tat" downward spiral that characterizes so many divorces and the world in general. Finally, I realized that the only person I could change was me. I decided to focus on identifying the things that God wanted me to change in myself, and not the things I wanted my wife to change in herself.

I shared these resolutions with my wife, but she was not impressed. Her lawyer told her that these were simply the empty words of a desperate man willing to say anything to avert a divorce and financial loss.

After Diane told me she was leaving, she lived in our house for another three weeks while searching for a place for her and our thirteen-year-old daughter, Shannon, to live. This made for many uncomfortable moments. Most notably were the times when I had some sort of admission or idea I wanted to share with my best friend. The problem was that my best friend was my wife and she was no longer accessible to me. She was the one who had set the divorce proceedings in motion and was not interested in hearing anything I had to say.

Three weeks after Diane pointed me to her lawyer, I found myself sitting in a courtroom for a *pendente lite* hearing. Diane was seeking temporary alimony and child support that would enable her to move out of our home and pay her bills while we worked toward a final divorce decree. The courtroom was filled with people who were seeking similar relief from the judge. One after another, couples were called before the bench and their attorneys slugged it out for fifteen minutes. Then the judge decided on the matter, and the bailiff called forward the next couple. The whole scene was sad and depressing. I wondered how I had reached this point.

Eventually our names were called. Diane was put on the stand and questioned by both of our attorneys. Then I was seated and questioned. Then the judge ruled. It was over in fifteen minutes, but it felt like thirty seconds. In the end, the judge ordered me to pay thousands of dollars of monthly alimony and child support to Diane, even though I had no income, and all our bank accounts were frozen except one. The one unfrozen account was nearly drained by my own lawyer's retainer fees.

As I left the courtroom, I suddenly realized my wife had invited some of her friends over to our house that night to pack her and Shannon's belongings. I had been so focused on preparing for the trial and working through the initial shock of the divorce that I hadn't even considered where I would stay while they were packing. There was no way I could go home that evening.

I decided to go to my parents' home, a small condo about twenty minutes from our house, to sleep on the floor. My dad was in his late seventies, my mom in her early eighties, and they were both in poor health. My mom was also quite a character. She had been one of the first policewomen in the city of Baltimore back in the 1950s, and she could be very combative. As we talked that evening, she said a lot of things about me that I didn't like. Hard things. True things. Things I needed to hear. She talked about my anger, selfishness, and overbearing nature. She talked about how I hurt people.

Of course, when people close to us tell us things that hurt, it's a natural reaction for us to get mad and highlight all *their* faults because it moves the spotlight away from us. At one point, I got so angry and offended that I jumped up from my chair, walked to the front door and grabbed the handle. I threatened to leave.

I'll never forget what happened next. My dad, who was usually uninvolved in conversations between my mother and me, had been sitting on the other side of the condo listening to us go at it. As I stood at the door, he rose and shuffled his unsteady body across the living and dining rooms. When he got close to me, he hugged me, told me he loved me, and pleaded with me to stay. We embraced, weeping. My mom cried too. I wound up staying.

The next morning, I got up early after a sleepless night on the floor. My parents were up as well, hobbling around, trying to help me in any way they could. They kept handing me twenty-dollar bills. I thought, *Based on yesterday's court ruling, I need way more than a few twenty-dollar bills*. Still, it was very sweet of them, and I took the money.

I got to my house that morning around 6:00 a.m. I entered through the garage door and found my wife at the kitchen sink. Standing about six feet from her, I told her I didn't think the court ruling was fair, but I wanted to honor my grace commitment. I then told her I was going to help her move. She didn't say a word or react in any other way, so I immediately got to work. I started breaking down the kitchen iMac and some other electronics. I loaded them in my car and headed to her new place. I met with the utilities folks that she had scheduled and got all her services up and running.

I would eventually drive back and forth between our house and Diane's new apartment four times to transport delicate items, tackle issues that arose, and do whatever was needed. At one point I got a call from a neighbor who asked, "Why is there a moving truck in your driveway?" This immediately reduced me to tears. Since I was standing near Diane when the call came in, I left her apartment and went down the hall to talk. I explained what was happening and hung up, eventually composed myself, and got back to work. Ten hours later the move was finished. I tipped the movers, sent them on their way, and found myself standing in the living room of Diane's new apartment. Our daughter was in her new bedroom on one side, and my wife was in hers on the other.

It occurred to me that this was unusual. Usually, a spouse who leaves wants to get far away from the other spouse and perhaps not even leave a forwarding address, yet here I was, standing in Diane's new apartment.

I went into my daughter's room to say goodbye. The moment was gut-wrenching. I remember very little of what we said, probably because it was so painful. Then I went to my wife's bedroom. She was standing at the far side of the room, facing me. I walked up to her and said, "I love you and I'm proud of you." I was shocked at the words coming out of my mouth. My human nature wanted to scream, "Look what you've done to me?! Look at what you're doing to our family!! How could you do this?!" Yet I felt compelled to say something radically different—something that wasn't focused on her and the bad things I thought she was doing, but rather on an unconditional and shocking expression of love and grace. I then gave her a hug and a kiss on her forehead. She was speechless. Saying nothing else, I turned away and left the apartment. I felt horrible walking down the hallway to the garage. I knew I was heading back to an empty home.

To this day, I'm still blown away by what I said and how I behaved. I'm utterly convinced that God spoke through me as a reward for my persistent prayers and strong desire to genuinely change. He moved me to say words I hadn't said in years, words my wife dearly wanted and needed to hear.

I drove back to our house, walked in the door, and was greeted by a huge mess—the result of a 24-hour packing and moving blitzkrieg during a daylong driving rain. Besides the tape, clothes, and household items that were strewn everywhere, water and mud from the mover's shoes had collected in many places. Despite not sleeping for thirty-six hours and being exhausted, I couldn't go to bed with the house in that shape, so I cleaned and straightened the first and second floors for several hours. Then I crawled into bed and passed out.

When I woke up the next day, it was surreal. My wife and daughter were gone, along with half of everything in the house, and things were still quite a mess. When I walked into my closet, I found it half empty, which was a jolt. I experienced the same reaction when I saw Shannon's empty closet. Then I went downstairs and noticed that sound echoed in the living and dining rooms because there was so little furniture left in them. I was heartbroken.

Somehow, I slogged through the day, moving from one straightening or cleaning task to another. At one point, the neighbor who had called me the day before stopped by with her new husband to offer support and encouragement. Her husband had been divorced six years earlier after a long marriage and raising three kids. He had lots of advice, including warning me not to get involved with other women as I worked through the months and years ahead. I took his advice seriously.

Later in the day, at around 4:00 p.m., something surprising happened. My wife called me. After we exchanged greetings, she began to describe how difficult things had been for her through the separation process while juggling her job, graduate school, and caring for our daughter. I was amazed. Once again, my human nature wanted to point out the toll her decision was taking on our family and me, but I remained silent and listened to her.

When she had finished sharing her difficulties, she mentioned that there was no food in her apartment, and that it was Mother's Day. Understandably, I had forgotten Mother's Day. She then asked if I would bring Shannon and her a pizza. I was shocked. I wanted to say, "Are you *kidding* me?! You want me to bring you a *pizza* after everything that's happened?!" But I also found myself feeling happy and thankful for the opportunity to serve my daughter and my wife.

I told her I'd be glad to bring them dinner and asked her to call her favorite local restaurant and place a carry-out order. She hesitated, as if she realized how strange this all seemed. I sensed her pause and reassured her that I was happy to help. We agreed on our plan.

I was pretty excited when I hung up the phone. I grabbed a house-warming gift I had bought for her—a compact tool kit—and ran out to my car in the garage. I then realized I had forgotten something, put the gift down on the floor of the garage, and ran back inside. When I returned to the garage and pulled my car out, I promptly drove over the tool kit. I got out of the car and inspected the damage. The kit had fared amazingly well, so I tossed it in the car and split.

It was pouring rain again, and I got totally drenched picking up our meals and getting into the apartment building. I didn't care. I was excited to have another chance to extend grace. When I arrived at her apartment, Diane had set the table. We unpacked our food, sat down together, and ate dinner as a family. I don't remember a lot of the specifics about our dinner together, except that it struck me as strange. What I do remember is what happened when I went to leave. As I stood at the front door and said goodbye, Diane walked up to me sheepishly, thanked me for bringing them dinner, and hugged me. I was stunned and hugged her back.

As we stood there with our arms around each other, thoughts flooded my mind. I first thought, *I've been pounding on this dear woman for years trying to change her into something I wanted, and it brought me to the brink of divorce and likely financial ruin. Now, after two days of extending genuine grace, she's hugging me.* I then thought of Jesus Christ and the sacrifice He made for us—one that doesn't require our worthiness or performance. In a flash, I understood the Gospel like I never had before. This was a revelation bigger than any I've had in my life.

Little more was said, except that I told her I loved her as I went out the door. Once I was in the hallway and the door closed behind me, I looked up toward heaven and told God, "I'm all in! I'm going to build my life on Your grace, and only grace, from now on, for the rest of my life."

3 | Too Much Information

Do not breathe the spray.

Warning label on an air freshener bottle

There is something about sickness and suffering that elicits a strong reaction from people. Our health is very near and dear to us because it has such a visceral impact on the quality of our lives. People have lots to say about it, and they do so with passion.

As we embarked on Diane's cancer journey, I soon realized that there would be no end to the number of opinions we would hear about what Diane should and shouldn't do. Our initial reaction to facing such a serious health threat was to throw ourselves into researching any and all possible treatments. It seemed that information and disinformation grew exponentially the more we dug. It became ridiculous and overwhelming.

Since I believe that the Bible is the ultimate source of wisdom for everything we encounter, I went to it first. I soon discovered that there were hundreds of passages that either described specific healing accounts, mentioned healing and/or health, or seemed related to health and healing without specifically saying so. I also found numerous books about healing in the Bible, but none of those I looked at gathered all the passages together in one place and performed a comprehensive analysis of them.

When it comes to miraculous healing, the range of opinions spans from those who believe that such healings don't happen anymore to those who say anyone can be healed if he has enough faith. In the face of these varying viewpoints, I wondered if anybody had ever performed a data analysis on all the Biblical passages that describe healing accounts. Without even thinking about it, I started capturing passages in a spreadsheet.

In parallel with my scriptural research, Diane and I began researching conventional options. We looked at surgical, chemo, and radiation treatments. We also tried to find and decipher clinical trial options and discovered it is hard for lay people to do. When we finally stumbled across *clinicaltrials.gov*, we were both impressed and dumfounded. We were impressed because we could search for trials based on cancer type, location, and other factors. We were dumbfounded because reading the descriptions of the trials left our heads spinning. We are neither doctors nor research scientists, and the jargon is unapproachable. It seemed impossible to determine which trials were a good match for Diane, and Diane's doctor kept saying trials should not be considered until she had exhausted the standard chemo treatment protocols.

I also began to search more deeply for "alternative" therapies. There seemed to be countless options to consider: Anti-angiogenic diets, Gerson therapy, cannabis, hemp, CBD oil, Essiac tea, the Harry Hoxsey therapy, Iscador/mistletoe, vitamin B17 therapy, dichloroacetic acid, shark cartilage, tocotrienols/vitamin E, vitamin D therapy, vitamin C therapy, herbal remedies, essential oils, Rife technology, Dimethyl sulfoxide, electro-medicine, antineoplastons, pancreatic enzymes, metabolic therapies, etc. The list went on and on. It seemed difficult if not impossible to figure out what could potentially work, who could be trusted to help us, and what stories could be believed.

What made matters worse was that many people seem to fall into extreme camps of faith healing, traditional medicine, and natural remedies. Western/conventional doctors often call the alternative folks "quacks" and "kooks." Alternative treatment proponents claim that all Western medicine can offer is poison, slashing, and burning via chemo, surgery, and radiation. And most people look at you like you have a hole in your head when you mention miraculous healing. These extremist views made it difficult to get a sense for what approaches are good, which are bad, and whether some combination of Western, alternative, and faith healing might work.

I got the feeling that by the time we gained some measure of understanding and control over all this information, Diane could be gone. There was simply no shortage of advice and opinions, with countless dimensions and layers of complexity.

Things got even nuttier when we started looking into the causes of cancer to identify foods, chemicals, and other things we should be avoiding. It turns out that the number of toxins in our environment and food is simply staggering. There are over 84,000 chemicals being used in the United States, and only 200 of them have been tested by the EPA.[3] These chemicals are everywhere. They're in our foods via pesticides, insecticides, fungicides, herbicides, food dyes, thickeners, hormones, and antibiotics; personal care products via Formaldehyde and fragrances, which can include any of 3,000 chemicals and aren't subject to labeling requirements; our furniture and furnishings via flame retardants, Phthalates, and PFCs; and household cleaners, which current laws exclude from labeling requirements.

I watched a TV program on CNN where the host got a Body Burden Test to see what his toxic load was.[4] They tested him for 28 chemicals and all of them were found in his body—some at alarmingly high levels. He purged his home of all sorts of offending products, including some major pieces of furniture and rugs; traveled around with a gas mask; and took all sorts of other precautions. Ten days later, he still had too many chemicals in his system. In a funny segment filmed while he was shopping for new personal and home care products, he noted that one air freshener warned, "Do not breathe the spray."

I have heard the term "toxic load" come up many times. People seem to realize that our bodies are taking in more and more toxins

---

[3] https://www.alternet.org/environment/84000-chemicals-use-humanity-only-1-percent-have-been-safely-tested.

[4] The Truth About Toxins, Morgan Spurlock Inside Man, Season 4, Episode 5.

as the years go by, and that we're increasingly likely to reach some sort of breaking point. You could draw analogies to a glass filling with water faster than it was being drained and the *I Love Lucy* episode where there aren't enough workers on a chocolate candy conveyor belt. Perhaps this "toxic load" partially explains things like the rising incidence of cancers and other diseases, and the increase in childhood ailments like asthma, ADHD, and autism.

On and on our research seemed to go. It soon became clear that Diane would simply have to pick something based on our knowledge at the time and dive in while we prayed and hoped for the best.

4 | Sweet Diane

Dear MB:[5]

Thank you for always being so loving and kind to me. For always being there when I need someone to talk to. For always being so generous and giving. In short, thank you for being such a wonderful mother-in-law. I truly appreciate all you do for me. Without having my own mother to turn to, your love and guidance has been invaluable to me. You make a difference in my life and I can't thank you enough for that. You are truly a blessing to me, and I love you very much. Diane

Mother's Day note from Diane to my mom
Approximately 6 years after our divorce

I first saw Diane as she walked through the student union building at Towson State University in the late 1970s. She was pretty, petite, well-built, and dressed nicer than most female college students. She was walking quickly in her dress slacks and heels while holding the hand of a tall, muscular guy. While I was attracted to her, I made a mental note that she was dating someone and turned my attention to other co-eds.

While we eventually wound up taking the same class at one point, she was still dating the big guy, and we never struck up a conversation during college.

After I graduated in 1982, I moved to Collingswood, New Jersey, to work with a small engineering firm that provided services to the first cellular telephone network operators. This was right at

[5] "MB" was a term of endearment that we used for my mom. While the origins are not certain, it's believed to be an acronym for Marge Baby as well as Main Brain.

the advent of commercial wireless communications, and I was traveling the country doing antenna site acquisition work. It was a cool job for a young, single person, but I soon tired of eating dinner alone every night in Holiday Inn restaurants. I really wanted to share my travel experiences with someone.

I had grown frustrated with the dating scene, though, and decided to stop thinking about finding a soulmate. I drove to my parents' house in Towson, Maryland, almost every weekend to get away from the roach-infested apartment I was living in, visit my college friends, and pop into my favorite nighttime haunts. It was on one of those weekends in late 1982 that Diane's and my relationship began.

I was in a bar called Poor Richards, drinking beers with a handful of friends as I had countless times during college. I was standing in the middle of a large crowd, somewhat removed from my buddies, when Diane suddenly appeared and started talking to me. I was a little startled. Seldom did pretty girls walk up and start talking to me.

She seemed determined to chat with me, and we exchanged pleasantries for a few minutes. At the end of our talk, she suggested getting together sometime in the future. I told her I would grab a matchbook and pen and jot down her number, but she said she would prefer that I memorize it. It turns out that she was there on a date and didn't want him to know that she was hitting on someone else.

She recited her number and I watched as she returned to her date and the two of them left the bar together. Then I made an urgent push through the crowd to get that matchbook and pen from the bartender. To be frank, I'm surprised I remembered the number. I had consumed quite a bit of alcohol.

I didn't call Diane for about three months following that brief conversation. I was traveling a lot, often one or two weeks at a time, and I had moved into a cozy, bug-free apartment on the top floor of an elderly woman's home.

When I finally did get around to calling her, Diane asked where I had been. She seemed put off and suspicious by the delay. Once I explained my work and living circumstances, however, she seemed satisfied.

We began dating in mid-March and within three or four months we realized we were madly in love. I was convinced we would spend the rest of our lives together.

I returned to Towson every Friday night to see Diane, and we would always have the best time together all weekend long. I got *so* bummed every Sunday evening as I headed back to New Jersey.

I bounded into work on Monday mornings, excitedly sharing what a great time I had had over the weekend. One of my co-workers would tease, "He's in love. He's in love," and imitate me coming down the hallway.

As the months passed, Diane started coming up to stay with me on weekends, and we eventually moved in together. We were engaged on Christmas Eve, 1984, and married on November 2, 1985.

Born Again

In March 1985, I went to lunch with a coworker and a salesman who was visiting our office. By that time, I was working at a satellite communications company in Rockville, Maryland. Diane and I had moved to Bethesda, Maryland, so I could go to graduate school at night in Washington, D.C., while we both worked full time.

The meal was unremarkable until my lunchmates started talking about a funeral they had recently attended for a mutual friend of theirs. My co-worker noted that, while everyone at the service was sad about their friend's death, most people were confident that they would see him again—which made the experience much more positive. When I asked him why this was the case, they began to explain their Christian faith to me.

It's worth noting that I had grown up in a decidedly non-religious home, the son of an atheist father and a formerly Catholic mother. My mom occasionally took my brother and me to church on Christmas Eve, but that was the full extent of our family's religious practices. No one at my house was reading the Bible, or praying, or doing anything else that I might expect a Christian to do. I was also the first person to flee from that strange guy on our college campus who wanted to share Jesus with me while I was trying to get to class.

I had always had a curiosity about spiritual matters but had never met anyone who seemed to know what they were talking about. Now I found myself conversing with two clearly knowledgeable and confident people in their twenties. They weren't trying to sell me on something or push me into any decision. They simply explained the Gospel and how I would live in God's perfect Kingdom for eternity if I simply acknowledged my sinfulness and accepted the sacrifice of Jesus Christ as payment for the penalty for my transgressions.

They patiently answered my questions as I probed their Christian faith. Then we got up and returned to work without any fanfare.

Later that day, I left work early to go home and watch a college basketball game on TV. I found myself alone in my large living room prior to the start of the game. I had been thinking about what my colleagues shared with me at lunch, and suddenly I decided to drop to my knees behind the sofa in the middle of the room and say a prayer. With my elbows propped on the rear edge of the sofa, and my head bowed, I shared with God what I had heard that day. I confessed my sins and accepted Jesus as my Lord and Savior. I ended by basically saying, "If what I heard today is true, please show me in an undeniable way."

Then I stood up, gathered a drink and snack, and turned on the TV. There were no angels singing, no overwhelming feelings of joy, no nothing. That was my big moment of conversion to the Christian faith.

When Diane came home later that night, I shared my experience with her. I don't recall her precise reaction. She didn't immediately drop to her knees, but she didn't react negatively, either.

Diane had also grown up in a non-religious family. Her dad seemed like the rebel in an otherwise devoutly Catholic family. Her mom was a complete atheist.

I eventually read a Christian book or two, purchased a Bible and began reading it, and I shared what I was learning with Diane as I went along. We started looking for a church to attend, and I eventually came across a global organization that had two congregations in the Washington, D.C. metro area. We connected with them, began attending services, and were baptized together within a year.

Change

After Diane and I moved to DC, our lives began to change. We began a six-year period during which we both worked full time and I attended graduate school at night. I had managed to get accepted into a master's degree program in electrical engineering and computer science despite not having a technical undergraduate degree. I wound up taking twenty-two classes instead of the usual eleven, and I was terribly unprepared for the advanced nature of the work, spending much of my time outside of my job studying.

To make matters worse, Diane's father passed away not long after we were married, and her mom sued Diane not long after that. Her dad had named Diane as a Personal Representative of his estate in the waning months of his life, and her mom was not happy about that. This sparked an ugly, eighteen-month battle in and out of various courts in Towson, which was an hour-and-a-half drive from where we lived and worked.

This was a very difficult time and, while our relationship remained strong, we quickly reached the point where we seldom relaxed and had fun. Things continued this way until I finally graduated, took a new job, and we moved to Paris, France, for three months for my job. The good news is that Diane could stop working for a while and recover from our legal battles and overworked lives. The bad news is that those three months represented the worst period in my entire career, and I took quite a bit of my frustration out on Diane. I was frequently in a bad mood when I came home from work and took my anger out on her by questioning and criticizing her for what she had or hadn't done while I was at work.

Shockingly, we decided to return to Paris for just over a year after my three-month assignment was over. I continued to struggle at work for a host of reasons—many of them my fault. I was often negative, easily offended, and dwelt far too often on what I perceived as slights and wrongs committed against me. My behavior was very un-Christlike.

Toward the end of our second stay in Paris, my manager informed me that no one at my company wanted me on their team when I returned to the U.S. This was incredibly sobering news, especially given the fact that he delivered it with such glee.

But here's the coolest part. I couldn't wait to get home that night, share what had happened to me, and receive Diane's unconditional love. And that's exactly what happened. I came in the door and cried my eyes out, and she tenderly hugged me. Then she listened to me and helped me work things out.

It was at this point that I determined to start examining myself so that I could identify and change whatever I was doing wrong at work. I never wanted to have another conversation like the one I had had with my manager that day.

Sweet Diane

As my relationship with Diane grew over the years, certain things about her stood out. The first was that she was incredibly gracious and kind to people of all backgrounds, and she was always willing to serve. My dad referred to her as "Sweet Diane" because of her ever-present smile, kindness to him and others, and thoughtfulness.

I can remember countless times when she extended kindness to people. I remember her tenderly holding the hand of a poor, elderly African American man we had just met at church, giving him her complete attention and respect.

Another example was the way she loved and worked with children with autism as part of her profession. When we were first dating, she would often meet me at the end of the work week bruised and battered from some of the more violent children, yet she was always overjoyed and anxious to talk about them, never commenting on her own injuries.

She was also incredibly accepting of my weaknesses and me. There was a time when something highly unusual and embarrassing happened to me in a public setting—something I was thankfully able to hide with some effort. When I saw her soon after, she unconditionally welcomed me with love, support, and acceptance. This issue would resurface many times over the years, and Diane never criticized me or made me feel unworthy.

Other words also come to mind when I think of Diane: hardworking, fun, stubborn, and determined. One weekend night during the first year of our relationship, we returned to her parents' house after drinking quite a bit. Her parents were away on vacation, and we were happy to have the house alone. Unfortunately, Diane had misplaced her key, and we couldn't get inside. Even after eventually opening the garage door, we still couldn't get through the door separating the garage and the basement.

It was at this point that Diane handed me a large ax and told me to break into her house. I didn't feel right about that, so I started lightly tapping on the doorknob with the blunt end of the ax, hoping to break off the knob. After a few moments, five-foot-three, one-hundred-and-fifteen-pound Diane grabbed the ax out of my hands, pushed me aside, and started wailing away at the door. She eventually chopped a hole in it, reached her hand through, and unlocked the door.

Her parents came home the next day and found the door with a hole in it. I'll never forget her father's reaction when he saw us later that evening. He just kept shaking his head and saying, "It just doesn't make any sense."

Diane's stubbornness was a recurring theme over the years, and it was especially obvious when she decided to leave me.

In the weeks and months following our separation, I also thought about Diane's graciousness, kindness, and acceptance. It occurred to me that I was on the verge of losing something of great value. While she wasn't perfect or blameless in the demise of our marriage, she was a true sweetheart, and I now yearned to extend the same grace to her that she had so freely given to me over the years.

5 | A Grim Prognosis

It was nice having your company. I'm glad you're helping with all this. I'm sorry it's taking a toll on your health. I accept whatever God has in store for me. I don't give up on doing whatever we can to restore my health, but I'll do my best to accept my fate with grace. I'm grateful for every day and your help seeing me through this. Just watched *Ratatouille* and dozed a bit! Now for the last piece of ricotta cake!

Text message from Diane to me
Late November 2016

Four months after her diagnosis, Diane and I traveled to Baltimore for a CT scan and a chat with her surgeon at The Johns Hopkins Hospital. Diane had completed five rounds of a highly toxic chemotherapy regimen known as Folfirinox and we were anxious to see the results of a new scan.

When the surgeon came into the consult room to chat about the scan results, he was more measured than in the past. This was a far cry from the first time we met him when he was brimming with confidence and bravado.

He said he saw some things in the scan that he didn't like, but that they were a little unclear and he wanted to have his best radiologist look at the results later in the week. He was so wishy washy that Diane finally said, "You do this all the time, so just say it." The doctor then revealed that he thought the cancer had spread to Diane's omentum, rendering her inoperable. When pressed harder by us, he said he was unaware of anyone who had ever been cured of pancreatic cancer with just chemo or chemo plus radiation. He said that surgery is always part of the treatment for people who are eventually cured.

The surgeon ordered a positron emission tomography (PET) scan, which is more effective at "lighting up" tumors than a CT scan. Diane then had me take a photo of her with him, and we headed home with instructions to see her oncologist following the PET scan. She really got a charge out of the surgeon. I thought he was a bit of a gas bag.

Despite the inconvenience of a long day, very bad news, the constant threat of diarrhea for Diane, and other issues, an amazing thing happened as I was leaving her apartment that night. All I could think was that it had been a great day. I told her how I felt, and she said she strangely thought the same thing. Can you believe that? We both felt surprisingly good.

When we later read the CT scan report, it said that her results were highly suspicious for something called peritoneal carcinomatosis (PC). While searching the Web, Diane found a 2013 study that determined that the median survival time for patients with PC was only 6 weeks, with a 95 percent probability of death within a five-to-seven-week window.[6] We were shocked at how little time she might have left.

Diane said the prognosis allowed for a greater miracle to occur. I challenged her to seriously think about what kind of life she would live if she were to survive this. I also asked her about something she said to me in the kitchen of our house ten or eleven years earlier when, unbeknownst to me, she was planning to file for divorce. She said she didn't care if she ever went to church again. She now said she didn't remember saying that and didn't feel that way now. She said she was at peace with God. I was so happy to hear those words. I'm convinced that much of her thinking just prior to our separation was formed by my poor behavior and example in the marriage. I was really glad to see that grace had brought us to a much better place.

---

[6] https://www.ncbi.nlm.nih.gov/pubmed/22850624.

Confirmation

Eight days after our meeting with the surgeon, and with Diane's scan reports in hand, we headed out to meet her oncologist.

Before the meeting, Diane was teasing that her PET scan had probably lit up like a Christmas tree. I wondered aloud if the highlighted parts were shaped like a tree. It was the holiday season. You gotta' laugh.

I said that she should try alternative remedies instead of more toxins, and she answered by saying she didn't have faith in such an approach but that she did have faith in God.

Shortly after the oncologist came into the examining room, he informed us that Diane's cancer had spread, that surgery was no longer an option, and that Diane was transitioning from a curative to a palliative mode.

We mentioned the PC study and asked if he felt she had only six weeks to live. He didn't answer the question immediately. Instead, he asked questions about Diane's pain and other symptoms. When he finished, he said he felt she would probably live three months. While this was better than six weeks, it was still shocking to hear such a short survival window.

He suggested that Diane switch over to the only other chemo option they offered: Gemzar-Abraxane. We had discussed the failure of Folfirinox despite its heavy toxicity and nasty side effects, and I again urged Diane to stop chemotherapy and focus on building up her immune system.

Diane's previous three months on Folfirinox had been extremely unpleasant to say the least. She suffered from a whole host of side effects which worsened with each treatment. These included, but were not limited to: extreme sensitivity to cold in her mouth and hands, making it painful to touch and taste things; extreme jaw pain with her first bites of food the first few days after treatment; neuropathy in her hands and feet; difficulty using her hands to do the simplest things, like turning on a lamp, opening lids, and manipulating zippers and buttons; difficulty controlling her tongue and talking; serious peeling of her thumb-tip and fingertip skin; fatigue and weakness; fever; swelling; breathing issues; near complete hair loss after only two treatments despite two nurses saying it would not happen; pain in her eyes when they teared up; diarrhea, including one spell that kept her in her apartment for nine days; and constipation. Diane was living alone, so dealing with these issues was rough. We had decided to let our daughter return to college in Brooklyn just a couple of weeks after Diane's diagnosis. I am frankly amazed at how strong Diane was through that period while living alone.

On one occasion early in her treatment, I got a phone call from Diane at about 9:30 at night saying she had collapsed on her apartment patio. Thank God an apartment complex employee happened to be delivering flowers to her (that she had been unable to retrieve from the front office) via the courtyard at the rear of her apartment. He helped Diane up and into her apartment, positioned her on her sofa, and gave her the phone to call me. I quickly packed an overnight bag and headed to her. I think my presence alone made a huge difference. She recovered nicely from the fall and had a good night's sleep.

On other occasions, I had to hustle over to help her as she dealt with allergic reactions to the chemo drugs. More than once I had to pick her up, take her to have her chemo pump removed, and drive her back home. Doctors advised Diane not to drive because of her side effects.

Diane typically felt bad for ten out of every twelve days between infusions. In fact, *all* of Diane's issues during chemotherapy were due to chemo, not cancer. This isn't hard to comprehend when one considers the vast amount of toxic chemicals pumped into her. Her chemo session at the infusion center every two weeks typically lasted six hours. During those hours, a chemo infusion technician administered four different chemo drugs plus medications intended to counter the chemo side effects, like anti-nausea and anti-diarrhea medicines, Benadryl, and cortisone. The number of bags of chemo and medicine they pumped into her was alarming.

At the end of each session, a portable pump was attached to her to deliver more of the fourth chemo drug over the next forty-eight hours. Finally, when she returned the pump, she was given a Neulasta shot.

One particularly nasty chemo drug in the regimen was Irinotecan. Its most serious side effects are severe and possibly deadly diarrhea and extreme suppression of the immune system. I thought sarcastically, *That's good for healing*. It's a "boxed warning" drug, which is the strongest warning the FDA can issue, indicating that the medicine poses a significant risk of serious or even life-threatening reactions. Two of the other chemo drugs also came with boxed warnings about anaphylactic shock as well as sudden, widespread, and potentially severe and life-threatening allergic reactions. This was madness.

On one occasion, Diane became delirious at the end of her session at the infusion center. She was having trouble controlling her tongue, talking, and using her hands. Of course, the solution to everything seemed to be more drugs, so they quickly pumped 50 mg of Benadryl and 100 mg of cortisone directly into her chest port. Diane proceeded to mistake a crumb on the floor for a moving spider, and then drifted into a delirious state that caused her to cry from laughing so hard. At one point she said, "When the end comes, just give me whatever you just gave me again." I have to admit that her comment was funny, but I was also scared.

Despite all of this, Diane began a new and different chemo regimen in mid-December 2016. I was bummed, but I kept telling myself, *It's her life and her choice. My job is to simply extend consistent grace and support.*

Beautiful Moments

While the first four months of Diane's cancer journey were increasingly tough, they were also filled with beautiful moments. Not long after her diagnosis, we started looking for opportunities to unplug and enjoy time together, and good meals became a common theme. I fondly recall several meals combining excellent food, great atmosphere, and a sense of peace.

On one late-October evening, Diane prepared a delicious meal of flank steak, mashed potatoes, and salad—all exquisitely cooked and seasoned. She served it on the patio of her ground-floor apartment and used small battery-powered lanterns on the table and light strings on the patio railing for lighting. It was a beautiful, peaceful evening, and we enjoyed the food, weather, and each other.

We also enjoyed several relaxing meals following church on Sundays, and I found myself really looking forward to that time together. I believe God blessed those meals in a special way because He was pleased that we were together.

Far more important than meals, though, were some deeply personal moments we shared. One day after Thanksgiving 2016, I visited Diane to set up her Christmas tree and enjoy her amazing pancakes for lunch. As I prepared to leave, Diane sat on the couch and began to cry. I sat down next to her and put my left hand on her tummy and my right hand on her back and gave her gentle rubs while praying. I could feel the left side of her stomach was a bit bloated. This broke my heart because her dad suffered with bloating when he had pancreatic cancer. I was very emotional as well. At the end of my prayer I confessed my mistakes in our marriage and my deep regret. She told me not to feel bad.

I don't care how many times I have read, "So now there is no condemnation for those who belong to Christ Jesus" (Romans 8:1), there are times when I realize I screwed up so badly that I have to walk through those moments before the comfort of scripture can sink in and give me relief. This was one of those times.

A few days later, following another visit with her, Diane texted me the note I included at the start of this chapter. She would later talk about how cozy she felt in bed at times, and the wonder of taking a shower. This made me think of something an acquaintance shared with me. As he recovered from life-threatening-injuries he sustained in a car rollover accident, he described the "daze of grace" he felt as he realized just how beautiful the world is. Amazingly, at a low point in Diane's journey, she was experiencing this same, wonderful daze.

6 | Insidious Decline

Look! It's a bird! It's a plane! No! It's 600 planes flying over our frackin' house each day! How do you like this card? I couldn't resist it when I saw it. Well, I'm about one hour away from San Francisco and I thought I would write to you. The flight has been smooth. I did a lot of reading and I wrote a note to the Courtials. Then I realized we probably already gave them most of the same news in a new address card. Did we? Well, who cares?! The news that you are pregnant is good enough. ☺ I know you hate these. How about this? Better? Obviously, the altitude has gotten to me. I miss you terble!![7] Take care of your big behind[8] and hopefully I'll beat this letter home. I love you, I love you, I love you! You're the best, best, best!! Goodbye boo-boo. Ed (That's a pumpkin)

Letter from me to Diane on a card with a photo of
Dulles International Airport
Early spring, 1994

Defendant is extraordinarily verbally abusive without any provocation… Defendant repeatedly [uses] the term "f***" when addressing Plaintiff… Defendant blames Plaintiff, verbally and abusively, for everything that goes wrong with his life… There is no hope of reconciliation… Plaintiff prays that she be rewarded the following relief: (1) Sole legal and primary custody of the parties' minor child, both *pendente lite* and permanently, (2) Spousal

[7] "Terble" is the way my mom pronounced terrible. Diane and I were constantly saying it that way to each other in jest.
[8] A term of endearment.

support both *pendent lite* and permanently, (3) Child support both *pendent lite* and permanently.

Complaint for Divorce filed by Diane M. Melick
April 2008

A year-and-a-half after our return to the U.S. from Paris, I had a new job I loved. We moved into a brand-new house near Dulles Airport, Diane was pregnant, and we had decided she would be a stay-at-home mom. I wrote the note included at the beginning of this chapter to Diane while flying to California for a business trip. Everything seemed to be going great.

Fourteen years later, Diane's attorney filed a Petition for Divorce containing the excerpts also cited above. One has to ask, what happened in that time period that moved me from gushing with affection toward my wife to being called out for my abusive language and treatment of her in a divorce filing—a filing so aggressive that it asked for *sole* custody and *permanent* spousal support?

The answer to this is both simple and complicated. The simple explanation has to do with the human heart—*my* human heart. The Bible reveals that our hearts and human nature are deceitful, desperately wicked, and hostile to God.[9] It also reveals that we are all equally guilty of sin.[10]

Over those fourteen years, I slowly grew self-absorbed, judgmental, insensitive to Diane's struggles, and isolated from people, especially the type of friends who would have checked my thinking and behavior. I drifted in and out of my relationship with God, and when I thought I was close to Him I was actually self-righteous and deceived about the quality of that connection. I put on

[9] See Jeremiah 17:9, Romans 8:7, and Galatians 5:17.
[10] Romans 3:23-24, James 2:10.

a happy, Godly face outside of my home and an ugly one inside of it.

I didn't truly wake up until the shock of the divorce hit me. It took my wife filing for divorce, my best friend and our daughter moving out of our home, and all the emotional, relational, and financial strain that go along with those things to sufficiently comprehend my behavior.

The complicated explanation has to do with the combination of personality traits, life events and experiences, and attitudes and beliefs that made our relationship unique.

Like any couple, we had our differences. Diane was quiet and tended to keep her deepest thoughts to herself while I was loud and tended to share everything. Diane liked to hold on to things and was happy in a cluttered home while I was a minimalist who wanted to clear everything out. Diane was slow and methodical in everything she did, sometimes painfully so, while I prided myself as a man-of-action who got things done quickly.

During those years, many things happened over varying periods of time. We both drifted away from God when Shannon was born, I started making more money, and the church we were attending underwent a dramatic change.

Diane's focus shifted significantly when our daughter was born. I went from ten years of being the primary object of Diane's attention and affection to playing second fiddle. My selfish heart didn't like that, so I reacted poorly. I used to joke to people that, before Shannon was born, if I casually mentioned I needed something, it would be on my bed when I got home that evening, but after Shannon was born, I could show Diane my broken leg and she would hardly notice. These obnoxious comments drove Diane further away from me and the separation between us kept growing.

There were also other trials. After initially thriving in the new job I loved so much, I started slipping back into the negative patterns of behavior at work that I had struggled with in France and was unexpectedly forced out of the company by the CEO in early 1997.

After suddenly finding myself on the street, I began doing consulting work, much of it with startup companies. This launched a ten-year period of radical income swings and lots of worry.

I also started working at home most of the time, which turned out to be a particularly bad thing…perhaps the worst thing of all. I saw first-hand how Diane often struggled to get things done, and I responded with frustration and criticism rather than compassion and thoughtfulness.

By the time we reached the last two years of our marriage, Diane and I spent very little time alone together. We slept in separate rooms, and she made decisions completely on her own that affected our family. She decided to go back to work, attended school at night, started exercising regularly, and built an entirely new wardrobe. She also stopped going on vacations with Shannon and me, including the trips to my parents' home in Rehoboth Beach, Delaware, during Shannon's school breaks, trips we had cherished for many years.

These were all huge flashing red signals. If you're reading this and recognize any of these things in your relationship, you need to wake up NOW. I didn't because I was in a deep state of denial. Despite knowing that things were not good in our marriage, I was convinced that we would never get divorced.

Near the very end of our marriage, the red signals got even brighter. I would stumble across books like *The Sweet Potato Queens' Divorce Guide*, and Diane would make strange comments like, "You'll get what you want soon." These things broke my heart and sent me into an emotional panic, but I was *still* convinced that we would never separate, so I said nothing and kept praying.

My lawyer would later tell me that there are typically two timelines in a divorce. There is one person who has already mourned the death of the marriage, checked out mentally and emotionally, and is planning a new life. Then there's the person who is aware yet in denial of the severity of the situation, and then shocked when told that his or her spouse wants a divorce. Clearly, I was the second person. This is sobering even now. How could she have gone through such a process without me even realizing it?

The decline in my behavior happened insidiously over many years. I often wonder when the first day was that I left our house mad and didn't kiss Diane goodbye and tell her I loved her. I wish someone had pulled me from my car and kicked my a**. One angry day eventually turned into two, and two turned into three. On it went, until I reached the point where I was mad all the time and could barely offer Diane a kind word or a smile.

Just days after Diane said she was leaving me, I met with a marriage counselor at my church. I sat across from him for an hour-and-a-half, crying and telling him my sob story. When I finished, he very gently and wisely smacked me upside my head.

He pointed out several things he heard from me as I talked, including my obsession with money and my anger. He talked about the importance of figuring out the root causes of my misbehavior, expressing appreciation to Diane, and demonstrating real change in my life.

At the end of our meeting, he challenged me to do two things. He told me to ask God to show me what He wanted me to know about *me*, and to stop focusing on what I perceived as Diane's flaws. He also told me to ask God to help me see Diane through His graceful, forgiving eyes. I would go on to ask God for these things many times over the weeks, months, and years to come. That simple, repetitive act of obedience completely changed my life.

7 | Turning a Corner

> I dread going back on chemotherapy and enduring the side effects again and being constrained by the schedule of chemo every week for 3 weeks at a time, which prevents any opportunities to travel. I've agreed to try it since the doctors say it could extend my life expectancy and hold off pain from the tumors. But if the chemo makes me sick again, I don't want to do it. I am just now starting to feel a bit like my old self, eating well, gaining some weight back, and being able to go out when I want without diarrhea. My bowel movements even look normal again. [It's] very hard to go back on chemo as I start to recover from it and know my first chemo drug failed to work on my tumor and allowed the cancer to spread. What guarantees do I have this new chemo will work? [The] doctors can't say. It's hard to ignore what the doctors say is my only hope to extend my life. And it's hard to face going on chemo again and facing side effects.
>
> Diane's answer to a question on a doctor's intake form
> December 2016

The sides effects and failure of Diane's first wave of chemotherapy led her to seriously consider non-standard treatments. It all started when she stumbled across a television special about the benefits of Cannabidiol (CBD) in treating cancer and other illnesses. CBD is one of over 100 chemical compounds in cannabis that act on cannabinoid receptors in our cells. It's extracted from cannabis plants that have been designed to produce low levels of Tetrahydrocannabinol (THC)—the stuff that makes you high—and is, therefore, illegal. Diane began taking high-potency CBD oil every day in late November.

Diane figured this was a good time, i.e., just after halting Folfirinox, to see how something like CBD would work. The only issue I had was that her decision to start a second-line chemo regimen (Gemzar/Abraxane) alongside alternative therapies would mean we couldn't draw clear conclusions about the correlation between improved/declining health and any given treatment. I was psyched, though, that she was interested in trying things to promote good health instead of simply poisoning her system.

I had also read about the healing properties of Essiac Tea and ordered some so she could cook up a batch. In early December, she began drinking the tea each day as recommended. We were also referred to a gentleman who operated a clinical practice offering botanical medicine and nutritional therapeutics to cancer patients. He is one of the smartest, most unassuming people I have ever talked to. We filled out his incredibly thorough intake form and had a two-hour phone consult with him in mid-December. The opening excerpt of this chapter was Diane's answer to one of the form's questions.

One thing we liked about him was his balanced perspective. While he was critical of the treatment of cancer with cytotoxins, he was respectful of Diane's decision to undergo chemotherapy. He offered to put together an extensive regimen of supplements that were customized to each week of Diane's treatment cycle. She would take certain supplements during her first week of chemo, others during her second and third weeks, and another combination during her off weeks. These were fine-tuned to accomplish various results, like helping her body to recover from chemo during her off weeks.

Once Diane got cranking on the protocol, she took anywhere from 24 and 40 pills and drank a specially formulated smoothie every day. It was a lot to ingest. She said at times she didn't feel like eating anything after stuffing herself with all the supplements. The protocol included vitamins we were familiar with (vitamins B, C, D, and K), herbs we were just learning about (curcumin, mistletoe, and ginger), and other herbs we had never heard of before (Ligustrum, Japanese knotweed, and astragalus).

Leaving Brooklyn

Our daughter was finishing up her fall senior semester in fashion design at Pratt Institute in Brooklyn, New York, in mid-December. As if dealing with her mom's illness while living in another state weren't bad enough, she was having some serious problems at school. She, along with her professors, decided that it would be best for her to take a leave of absence for a year and finish one of her core fall classes at home in Virginia during the spring of 2017.

We were thrilled to welcome Shannon home to stay with her mom. So, I headed up to Brooklyn, packed everything she had in a rental van, and brought her home. We even brought home things she typically kept in storage, just in case something unforeseen happened and she didn't return to school.

South Beach

Diane started a three-plus-one (3+1) treatment regimen on December 12 which required chemo once per week for three weeks followed by an off week. This was a bummer for a number of reasons. Diane hadn't had chemo since November 16, and she was feeling better each passing day.

Just a day and a half after starting her new regimen, Diane had a 102-degree fever which touched off a day-long round of doctor and nurse visits and tests. In the end it turned out to be the chemo. I thought, *Here we go again.*

As we neared the end of December, Diane started talking about taking a trip during her off-week. She figured that if the doctors were right about how much time she had left, she should get as much fun in as possible in her final two months. We joked about movies in which someone is given a short time to live and they go on blowout trips and spending sprees. But a 3+1 regime would have her on chemo for most of every month, and likely recovering during the off week.

I agreed to pay for half of the trip, and we started thinking about possible destinations and calling travel agencies and hotels. Diane really wanted to go to Italy, and we talked about the Caribbean and sailboat tours.

After a while it occurred to us that we needed to pick a destination that was bookable on extremely short notice, allowed refunds on short notice, wasn't outside of the country or in the middle of the ocean, and was near major hospitals/medical facilities in case of an emergency.

Someone mentioned the 1Hotel in South Beach, Florida, to Diane. We checked it out on the Web, and it looked amazing—but the prices were ridiculous. I called them on December 28, the day of Diane's third treatment of her first new chemo cycle. The reservations rep gave us what nobody else would—that is, complete flexibility with our reservations. They said we could arrive late, or come and leave early, and we would only be billed for the nights we stayed. I was sold.

Now all we needed to do was pick the right room. The hotel was so expensive that I was leaning toward a studio—a room with no separate bedroom. Even though we were sharing the cost of the trip, my "cheap gene" was rearing its head. One night, at about eight o'clock, I was in Diane's apartment, and Diane and Shannon were both crashed on the floor. We had been debating the pros and cons of a separate bedroom for a while and there was an unexpected silence in our discussion. Then, suddenly, I let out a one-gun salute. There was another pause, and I said, "Let's get a separate bedroom!" We all broke out laughing.

I made the reservations on the 29th, booked plane tickets on the 30th, and we flew out of National Airport on New Year's Day 2017.

We arrived at our hotel at about 6:00 p.m. The room and hotel were amazing. Our one-bedroom suite had two bathrooms, an insane kitchen with every accoutrement you could think of, and—according to the valet—triple filtered water…including the toilets. This became a running joke throughout the trip.

We had a wonderful dinner and when we returned to our room, Shannon and I sat out on the balcony and marveled at the stars and surf. We got excited for the morning when we would discover what some of the dark shapes we were seeing on the shoreline actually were. The balcony became a favorite haunt of Shannon's on the trip—whether morning, mid-day, or evening.

We quickly settled into major chill mode over the ten days of the trip. Each morning, I got up before everyone and took a walk along a brick path which ran parallel to the beach. Sometimes I hit the hotel gym afterwards. Then I ate breakfast. Diane and Shannon got up later and I hung out with them while they ate. Then we wandered from poolside lounge chairs to the beach to the rooftop pool to the balcony of our room. We got most of our food from Whole Foods and a café in the lobby and ate it in the room. You know restaurant prices are outrageous when Whole Foods seems like a cheap alternative!

There was an occasional trip out to get food, or to shop for a bathing suit for Diane, or to take Shannon to urgent care for a double ankle injury she suffered in a nail salon in Little Haiti. But we mostly stayed on-site at the hotel.

The trip was really good for Diane. She noted that it was nice to get away from the atmosphere of cancer that seemed to be all around her back in Virginia. She said that everywhere she turned in her apartment, there was a reminder of her disease. Doctor bills, research papers, cancer books, devices to help her with side effects, growing mounds of drugs and supplements, etc. Everywhere she went, like her treatments, blood work appointments, doctor visits, support groups, cancer counselor meetings, etc., seemed to be related in some way to cancer. Most of those reminders were left behind, and the hotel room never felt ominous.

Diane was getting good sleep every night, which was unusual for her, she was with her daughter, and it was 70 to 80 degrees and sunny each day. Even the music by the pool was outstanding. I found myself constantly getting up from my poolside lounge chair to Sound Hound songs on my mobile phone. What a hardship!

There were several elements that stand out from the trip that are worth mentioning. First, no matter how much you try to get away from cancer, it follows you to some degree. Whether Diane was watching a TED talk on cancer in the hotel room, struggling to find the right bathing suit to cover her distended stomach, or tolerating people staring at her because of her baldness and hats, cancer was with us—even in paradise.

Second, there were several tender moments during the trip that I will never forget. They all came before bed. The first occurred a few nights into the trip, after I said a bedtime prayer with Shannon and Diane as they reclined on the king-size bed in their bedroom. After I left their room, Diane came out to me in the living room and gave me a very tender hug, unlike any she had given me for a long, long time. She stood on my left side with her right arm around my waist while her left hand gently rubbed my chest over my heart. A couple of nights later, Diane came out to me while I was passed out on the sofa bed, rubbed my back and gave me a kiss on the head. These moments were priceless.

Third, Diane was really impacted by a book I had given her called *A Reason for Hope* by Michael Barry, the former Director of Pastoral Care at the Cancer Treatment Centers of America in Philadelphia. She began reading it in December and brought it up during our trip on a couple of occasions. She was also moved by two young Christian women who visited her two days before our trip to pray over her and proclaim healing for her. She noted how nice it was reading and hearing words of hope and encouragement in those two contexts, and how that seemed to be the exception rather than the rule for people fighting cancer.

She began to realize how important hope is for healing. I had read my own copy of the book and was there when the young women visited her. I reached the same conclusion. Diane talked about how the doctors speak with so much gravity, glumness, and resignation. She was appreciative of them trying to be diplomatic and careful, but it bugged her that they were all so negative and assumed that she was headed in only one direction.

It's interesting to note that mainstream medicine is catching onto the importance of hope. My favorite example is something that renowned Harvard Medical School Professor Jerome Groopman wrote in his book, *The Anatomy of Hope*. He noted, "For all of my patients, hope, true hope, has proved as important as any medication I might prescribe or any procedure I might perform."[11]

One of the most important aspects of our trip was that we did very little on the trip except eat, rest, and spend lots of time together. We occasionally tried to go out, like when we went to a well-known Sunday market in the heart of South Beach one afternoon. After about ninety minutes, though, we all agreed we had had enough and headed back to the hotel. This was typical. After we got back to Virginia, when people asked me what we did for ten days, I basically said, "Nothing. And it was great."

February Scan

Diane and I visited her oncologist the day after we returned home from Miami, and she had chemo the day after that. Talk about cutting it close! The doctor was amazed at how good she looked. She weighed 117 pounds—up from a low of ninety-three during her first chemo regimen on Folfirinox. He also said her blood work looked good. We had him laughing with funny Miami stories, especially about the parade of impossibly hip/beautiful women at

---

[11] *The Anatomy of Hope*, Jerome Groopman, M.D., Random House, Inc., New York, 2005, page xiv.

the hotel, and South Beach in general. He said that the trip was the best thing Diane could have done for her health.

A few weeks later, after Diane finished her second three-week treatment cycle, we headed to New York City for three nights and stayed in a two-bedroom Airbnb penthouse apartment in SoHo. Shannon spent the next two days shopping for fabric for the class she was working to finish from home in Virginia. That left Diane and me alone for most of those days. We had a really nice time. Diane got good rest, we had lazy mornings, and we strolled SoHo each of the two full days. We somehow managed to find ourselves in Dean & Deluca way too many times, probably to get away from the cold. New York City in February was quite different than South Beach in January!

The day after we returned from New York, Diane had a CT scan and the results were surprising. After hearing nothing but glum predictions and reading terrible morbidity statistics, the cancer in her omentum had shrunk, and there was no evidence of new areas of metastasis.

Diane's oncologist was unusually happy when he came into the examining room. He said, "This must be the good-news room." I assumed another patient had good news there earlier in the day. Despite his giddiness, he still said "you have an incurable disease" twice during our appointment along with some other negative things. After reading the book about hope, Diane and I weren't having it. We shared with him our belief in the importance of a positive, hopeful attitude—no matter how delusional it might seem to others—and asked him to refrain from the negative talk as much as possible. He seemed to get the message and generally stopped saying such things in subsequent meetings.

Alone at the Beach

Seeing what a good effect the Miami and New York trips had on Diane and our family, I suggested we take a trip every month on her off weeks from treatment. They didn't have to be long trips or blowouts like Miami—just a change of scenery and refreshment.

Diane immediately took me up on that by going alone to my brother's beach house in Rehoboth Beach, Delaware, for a week at the beginning of March. I was kind of rattled by this and felt worried the entire time she was away. This was around the time the doctors had predicted she would no longer be with us, and I couldn't believe she was heading out of town alone for a week.

Shannon stayed behind to keep pushing through her schoolwork, which was due in April. I stayed behind because, frankly, I wasn't invited. At first, I was a little hurt by this. I enjoyed our time together in Miami and New York and was looking forward to more trips together. More than one friend suggested, though, that it could be exactly what Diane needed, whether she was aware of it or not. They thought that some time completely alone may be exactly what God wanted for her at that moment.

On her way home from the beach, she met Shannon at the MGM Theater at the National Harbor to see an Il Volo concert. I thought, *This woman is amazing*. The doctors figured she would either be dead or very sick by then, and there she was traveling alone for a week and popping by a concert on the way home.

Aside from some chemo side effects, Diane was functioning fairly well. The side effects were nothing to sneeze at, though, especially the neuropathy in her hands and feet which impacted her mobility and the use of her hands. The doctors told her that this condition could become permanent, and that it could very well be the result of the first chemo cocktail they gave her. I was dismayed by this news and wondered what other bad things lay in store for her down the road.

The Flood

On March 25th at about 4:00 a.m., my cell phone rang while I was sleeping. I looked at the caller ID, and it was Diane. I answered, but there was no one on the line.

I called her back. No answer. Then I sent Shannon and her a group text asking if they had called me. I didn't hear back from them, so I dozed off figuring that Diane had probably body-dialed me while rolling over her phone in bed.

At about 5:30 a.m., I got another call. This time it was Shannon. She said a water pipe had broken in the ceiling of their apartment. Long story short, their apartment was completely flooded. It turns out that Diane did, in fact, try to call me at 4:00 a.m., but her phone went dead the moment I answered. Then they quickly got swallowed up in the work of moving things out of the spreading water's path.

I jumped up, got dressed, and bolted out the door to join them. When I arrived, I realized how bad things were. Amazingly, I had experienced almost an identical flood in my condo just one year before when a worker triggered a sprinkler head in my laundry closet. I had lots of experience in flood remediation and knew what Diane and Shannon would go through.

The building complex manager and his remediation team immediately started to pressure Diane to move everything out of her apartment so they could tear up all the flooring, cut out the base boards, and set up industrial fans to dry out the unit. Of course, it was Friday afternoon when all this happened, and Diane's insurance company couldn't find anyone to move her stuff until the following Monday. So, I brokered a deal. I told the building manager that we would be out by close of business on Monday if they could find a place on-site for us to store Diane's stuff. They offered her an apartment down two long hallways from her current unit that was awaiting the arrival of a corporate tenant in a month or so.

We spent that entire first day shoveling and mopping water, moving stuff around, and watching the disaster recovery team rip out carpet, baseboards and drywall. I couldn't believe Diane and Shannon could even stand at the end of the day. Shannon had been up the entire night before doing schoolwork, and Diane was only two days removed from her last chemo treatment, which usually left her exhausted and feverish.

At the end of the day, I helped them gather their most important things into our two cars and brought them to my condo. We ate some leftovers for dinner, and we all got in bed at a decent time. I gave up my queen-size bed for Diane, and Shannon gave up her full-size bed for me—mainly because she passed out on the couch like a ton of bricks at 10:00 p.m.

In the end, Diane and I completely cleared out her apartment by 5:00 p.m. on Monday as promised—basically three-and-a-half days after the flood. It was insane. We had some help from a buff posse of teens, a friend of mine, and a dear friend of Diane's. But most of the work was done by Diane and me. The insurance company finally found some movers to help on Monday, but they did more complaining than good, and made some really bad decisions—like packing plant poisons with Diane's silverware.

Despite not being able to feel the bottoms of her feet, Diane killed herself during those three-plus days. What's even more amazing is that when we visited her oncologist on Tuesday, *the day after* all that action, her blood pressure and heart rate were better than they had been through six months of chemo. I looked at her and suggested that we flood *my* condo again so that she might get even better.

Diane and Shannon wound up living with me for twelve weeks while their new living arrangements could be ironed out. My condo went from a neat, uncluttered space to absolute chaos overnight. For the first five weeks, we couldn't even see the TV given the massive worktable Shannon set up in the middle of the living room to complete her fashion collection and the boatload of fabrics and sewing supplies that came with it. And then there was Diane's stuff.

While we had our moments, we really enjoyed living together. I felt great knowing that they were with me, safe and snug, and that I could help with everything from cleaning up after meals to encouraging them to relax and have fun.

Continuing to Improve

In mid-April, just three weeks after completely shutting down Diane's apartment, Diane and I accompanied Shannon on a trip to Brooklyn to support her as she presented her fall senior semester fashion collection to her professors. Though she had worked diligently, suffered with a mom battling cancer, cleaned out a home that was flooded, and endured teachers and peers who did not support her, her professors didn't seem as impressed as we were. She ended up with a grade of D+. We were less than thrilled, to say the least.

Diane and Shannon went away together on one more trip in May before moving into their own apartment in June. I did not want them to leave. I asked Diane to stay with me so I could take care of her if her health began to decline, but despite us getting along really well, she didn't feel completely at ease living in my place. She didn't have access to most of her belongings, and she felt bad about Shannon's and her things cluttering up my condo.

Diane had three more scans through October that all showed some combination of shrinkage and stability in both her tumor and metastasis. While this sounded great, a couple of things were chewing at me. First, Diane was on palliative care, meaning the doctors were planning to pump chemo into her system until she either couldn't tolerate it anymore or her cancer took a serious turn. Every time I thought about this approach to her care, it sickened me.

Second, I'm not naïve about what typically happens with patients fighting the deadliest cancers. Many appear to respond to their initial chemo treatments as their doctors hail the shrinkage of tumors. But the cancer almost always seems to come back, and suddenly the patients are gone. This is especially true of pancreatic cancer.

On the positive side, Diane was given three months to live at the end of November 2016, and here she was looking great one year later. We had moved from a state of sadness, fear, and worry to one of hope and gratitude.

I'm reminded of a couple of scriptures that I've been holding onto in my heart. In a letter to the church at Philippi, the Apostle Paul wrote, "And I trust that my life will bring honor to Christ, *whether I live or die*."[12] Also, in the book of Daniel, three of Daniel's friends are quoted as saying, "If we are thrown into the blazing furnace, the God whom we serve is able to save us… But even if He doesn't… we will never serve your gods."[13] *Whether I live or die…but even if He doesn't…*Those words resonated within me.

I gained a hopeful, yet realistic outlook from these scriptures. I decided that whether or not Diane's condition improved I would trust that all things would work out for the best.

---

[12] Philippians 1:20.

[13] Daniel 3:17-18.

8 | Growing Grace

> The head of the [teacher's] union couldn't believe you're my ex-husband. She hasn't talked to her ex in five years. I told her you do things like this because of the grace of Jesus Christ.

Diane's comments to me on the phone following
a meeting with the head of her teacher's union.
Spring 2011

Grace is basically the unmerited favor given to one person by another. The less worthy a person is of such favor, the more powerful it is when extended. The ultimate expression of grace occurred when Jesus died for mankind while we were still sinners—while we were his enemies. It was the utmost expression of God's love for us.[14]

Diane and I had become enemies toward the end of our marriage, and her filing for divorce kicked off a host of aggressive actions that rocked me to the core. Regardless, from the moment I left her new apartment on Mother's Day 2008, I determined to seize any and all opportunities to extend grace to her, no matter how she or her lawyer treated me throughout the divorce proceedings.

When I began sharing this with people, I was met with a chorus of criticism and mean-spirited advice. Many people told me I was stupid, that I was letting her abuse me, that I needed to get mean, and that I should cut off all communications between my family and her. I told them that such behavior was what led to my separation, and that I was going to try grace. Thank God there were a handful

[14] Romans 5:8.

of Christians who were applauding my decision and supporting my efforts.

The first weeks and months were rough on all three of us. I was devastated and found myself crying so intensely at times that I wondered if I could stop. I coined the term "deep tears" to describe this.

I didn't have a job or any consulting income and was faced with the cost of running our house while also paying thousands of dollars in monthly alimony and child support. Diane was a teacher's assistant making about $19,000 a year at the time, which must have factored into the judge's decision to hammer me.

My attorney urged me to meet an employment consultant who would assess my employability and earnings potential. Of course, this cost several thousand dollars, and the guy clearly had no understanding of what I did, how I acquired consulting contracts, or anything about my industry. *Some expert*, I thought.

I met with him very early in the separation when I was a wreck. After an hour or so together he expressed concern over my ability to pull myself together and behave professionally in an interview. I wondered what he was expecting from people like me. My life was falling apart, and he seemed to think I should be able to compose myself at the snap of a finger.

Everyone was pressing me to get a regular job, as if something like that simply fell out of the sky for a 46-year-old guy who had held some high-level positions in the past. I had landed my previous two jobs after working first as a consultant with the companies that hired me. Finding consulting work requires time, though, and I needed cash fast because most of our money was sitting in frozen bank accounts.

I soon realized I had fallen into the grips of the divorce industry. Everybody was pointing me to someone they told me I needed to see. They all wanted money, and they wanted it up front. They knew my lawyer was going to quickly devour what little cash I had, and they wanted to make sure they got paid before that happened.

This included the employment consultant. My lawyer insisted that I meet him, saying we needed an "expert" to tell the courts what a former consultant would typically earn in a full-time position. This was part of his strategy to lower my alimony and child support while I searched for work. After the failure of my attorney's initial strategy during the *pendente lite* hearing, I had little confidence in this one.

One of the awful things about divorce is that suddenly a whole bunch of people who know nothing about your life are telling you what it should look like. It's ridiculous.

But here's where something good happened to me. I was working on two consulting projects just prior to my separation—one full-time and the other about eight hours per week. I had been brought onto the part-time project by a local entrepreneur with whom I had worked in the past. He knew me well and respected my work, so he went to bat with the owners of the company I was consulting with and they offered me a good paying job.

I can't tell you how thankful I was. The employment consultant was shocked. He thought I would never land a gig given my fragile emotional state. He didn't think I could make it through the interview process. He was probably right.

Getting a Groove On

Things were strained on Diane's side as well. She was working a full-time job, was in school at night, and was trying to dig out from moving a ton of stuff from our house into her apartment. The silver lining for me was that she started asking me to help in several ways, especially by watching Shannon and often having her stay with me.

Now keep in mind as you read this that Diane's lawyer was asking for *permanent* alimony and *sole* custody of our daughter. Permanent alimony means that you receive alimony for as long as both people are still alive and the recipient does not remarry. In Virginia, the "guidance" that judges use when calculating alimony is half the duration of the marriage up to a twenty-year marriage.

There is no guidance for marriages longer than twenty years. So, there are cases in which someone who was married for nineteen years pays nine-and-a-half years of alimony, and someone married for twenty-one years winds up paying twenty, thirty or even more years of alimony. I was married for twenty-two-and-a-half years when Diane filed for divorce, so I was concerned how a judge might rule.

Also, a request for sole custody is typically reserved for situations where something especially serious is going on such as physical abuse. This was *not* the case. Shannon and I were very close and got along well. Diane's attorney appeared to be setting the bar high so she would have bargaining leverage down the road. According to my attorney, this was quite a slap in the face.

On top of this, a lot of bad things were said in the original divorce filing. Regardless of whether they were true or not (and most were), they were now on the public record. This was very embarrassing and shameful for me.

My lawyer kept asking me if we should file something that countered what was said. I was mad at first and started typing up all sorts of things. Then I remembered what I had said to Diane. No tit for tat. I had committed to extending grace and only grace. So, I decided not to file anything hostile then or throughout the entire ordeal—even though Diane's attorney continued to do so.

I also strove to be kind and loving whenever I saw my wife, which turned out to be quite a bit. There were lots of Shannon handoffs and times when Diane would ask me to come by her place and help with something. I found myself going over to her apartment complex to watch Shannon and her friends at the pool while Diane studied, to put together bedroom furniture my parents purchased for our daughter, and to bring over items Diane had neglected to take during the move.

On one occasion, Diane called and asked me if I could help her bring over a large desk that she had overlooked in our basement in her haste to move. I called my next-door neighbor and asked if I could borrow his truck. He said he would come and give me a hand carrying the desk.

The interesting thing about this is that my neighbor's wife had left him about a month before my wife left me. His separation was not going well and there was a lot of friction between his wife and him. He was surprised, even a little bugged, to see me helping Diane, but, to his credit, he dove in. There was an awkward moment after we had delivered and set up the desk and the three of us were standing in Diane's living room. I got the sense that my neighbor was studying us and the unusual dynamic of grace taking hold in our relationship. A month or so later, while I was visiting him, Diane even popped by to give me a gift that she had purchased for me while in New York with our daughter. I could tell that he couldn't quite make sense of what was happening.

I have many "grace stories" from the years following our separation. And some not-so-graceful ones…

The First Thanksgiving

A little over six months after Diane had moved out, Thanksgiving was upon us. The "grace" bug seemed to be catching on because my parents suggested that we—my parents, Diane, Shannon, and me—spend the holiday together as a family. I was all for this because I wanted any and all opportunities to be with Diane and Shannon. Surprisingly, Diane agreed to join us. We planned to meet at my parent's condo on Thanksgiving Day in the early afternoon. Diane agreed to do most of the cooking at her place and bring the already-prepared food to the condo.

Our plans were moving forward nicely until Thanksgiving morning arrived. While I can't remember exactly what triggered it, Diane and I wound up battling on the phone before either of us had left our homes for Nana and Granddad's place. We both hung up in anger and I thought our plans for the day were shot. I dropped to my seat on the floor of the foyer in our big, half-empty house. I was frustrated and sad and yelled, “Screw it and everyone! I’m not going over to my parent’s place! They can all do Thanksgiving without me!”

Then I thought of grace, and I wondered what, exactly, I would accomplish by getting mad and bailing on our celebration. I thought of my parents, who badly wanted to see their granddaughter, me, and even Diane. I thought of Shannon, my dear sweet girl. And I thought of Diane. I loved her and didn’t really want to hurt her—and I knew she had worked hard to prepare her typically great meal. So, I prayed, called Diane back and apologized, and said, “Let’s do this thing.” We did, and it was great. No one was pouting, frowning or acting like they were “doing it for the child.”

Since then, the three of us have spent almost every Thanksgiving and Christmas together as a family, as well as many other holidays. This was utterly baffling to most people in the early years of our separation/divorce, but that attitude is their loss.

The following Thanksgiving, just after our divorce was settled, my brother and his wife were in town and invited the family, including Diane, to their place. Before the meal, his wife asked everyone to say why they were thankful. Diane thanked everyone for letting her continue to be part of the family. There’s really no amount of alimony, grief, or hardship that could outweigh hearing such a beautiful thing. It was proof of the realness and power of God’s grace.

But, as I said, sometimes things weren’t so “graceful.”

A Low Point

The most jarring moment I experienced after Diane left our home occurred toward the end of the first year of our separation. We were approaching the trial date to determine a final divorce settlement, and there was a good deal of tension between us over what the outcome would be.

I was bringing Shannon back to Diane's apartment on a Sunday night after her weekly stay with me. Shannon had mentioned some problems they were having with their iMac, and I agreed to look at it. We knew Diane was not in the apartment. We also knew that the family computer had been a source of great frustration for me in the past. I think I purchased one of the few dud iMacs on the market, and nearly every time I wrestled with it while we were all living under the same roof, I ended up in a foul mood. I was glad that Diane would not be home when I tried to troubleshoot the device.

Shannon and I agreed to rush in the door, get right down to business, and hopefully wrap things up before Diane got home. Of course, things never go as smoothly as you hope when you're working on a computer, and I got bogged down. Before long, Diane came in the front door, which was right next to the computer. It was clear from the moment she arrived that she was very angry, and she was not pleased to see me working on her machine.

While I can't remember exactly what was said, what stood out was that she was focusing her anger on Shannon. This was a weak spot for me. I had been practicing extending grace to her for nearly a year and was getting pretty good at handling negative comments and actions. But this was different. Something about her picking on Shannon really got to me.

Diane started laying into her, and I started laying into Diane. We were positioned in a triangle with about eight feet separating each of us from the others. There was a lot of handwaving and yelling going on. At one point, Shannon dropped to her knees, crying and pleading with us to stop fighting. I pointed my finger at Diane and told her to stop yelling at Shannon. The implication was stop yelling at her *or else*.

And then it hit me. I realized the situation could easily escalate into something more serious, like a physical altercation. While this had never happened before, the thought rattled me, and I decided to leave the apartment immediately. I don't remember the last thing I said or how I did it, but I turned to the door and left.

I moved swiftly down the hallway of her floor, hopped in my car, and drove out of the garage and down the road. I was both pumped up and frightened, and I needed to talk to someone. I called the counseling pastor from my church whom I had been meeting with over the past year. I told him what had happened and asked for his advice. He said maybe it was best for Diane and me to steer clear of each other while we were going through this difficult period. He also suggested I own up to my role in the fight and apologize for it.

I felt bad about what happened and wanted to talk to Diane as soon as possible, so I hung up and immediately called her. I apologized and told her what the counselor had said. She apologized, too, and agreed.

I can't tell you how nice it was to quickly and humbly deal with the situation and come up with a solution for moving forward. It also occurred to me that sometimes grace involves staying away from someone, like in circumstances where tensions are high.

Negotiations

A few months after the incident in Diane's apartment, Diane, our lawyers, and I were scheduled to meet in her lawyer's office to bang out a settlement agreement. I was truly upset with what was about to happen and was on edge as I drove to meet my lawyer before the meeting. As I neared my destination, I was cut off by another car, and I responded by honking my horn and cursing. The driver, in turn, performed a jerk-off gesture and laughed. That was too much for me with what lay ahead of me that day.

As we drove through the small, old-town area of Fairfax City, he turned right into a narrow parking lot dividing a row of businesses. I passed the lot by ten or so feet, stopped my car in the left lane of the road, and rolled down my passenger window. I watched a man who looked to be about thirty years old get out of the car and walk toward the sidewalk near where I sat in my car. He clearly didn't know I was waiting.

I then unleashed a verbal tirade on him. He was startled, and he paused and said nothing. As I continued to unload, another car slowly pulled up between us, and I realized it was a policeman. The policeman told me to move on. I responded by yelling about what an awful thing the other driver had done. The policeman calmly responded by saying, "If you don't want to get arrested, move on."

I paused for a moment and began to grasp the situation I had gotten myself into. I slowly moved my car forward to the next traffic light, and the policeman passed me and stopped about a block down the road, watching me in his left rear-view mirror.

When my light turned green, I turned and drove the two blocks to my lawyer's office. When I parked my car, I was shaking and grieved. I cried out to God and asked Him to help me get through the next few hours in a way that was pleasing to Him. I had gotten extremely angry twice within a three-month period, and I felt like I was falling apart.

After I finally composed myself, I met my attorney and we headed over to Diane's lawyer's office together in his car. When we arrived, I was greeted by Diane's lawyer, who immediately had me deposed by someone wearing a stenographer's mask, a handheld microphone that looks like a fighter pilot's mask and can be unsettling when seen outside of a cockpit. This was not what I had envisioned or needed after the driving incident.

Diane's attorney seemed to be trying to catch me in a lie prior to the negotiation session. But I hadn't done anything wrong. In fact, I had gone out of my way to be completely honest with Diane about my finances and everything else related to the divorce. I kept reminding myself that many people do, in fact, lie, and that I should accept the deposition as a normal part of the process. The fact that I had nothing to hide calmed me.

We eventually sat down on opposite sides of a conference room table. Our lawyers started marching through the agreement while hashing out points with our input. I noticed they were writing the changes by hand on paper. I thought, *You have to be kidding me. In this age of laptops and computing, they aren't really doing this in ink, are they?*

I asked them if they wanted me to break out my laptop and capture the changes real-time. They declined and continued. After a few more minutes of watching them write things out via longhand, I asked again if I could help. Again, they said, "No."

At that point, I simply whipped out my laptop and started making changes to the version of the agreement I had read the night before. Within a few minutes, the lawyers were declaring what a great idea this was. For the next hour-and-a-half, we were a well-oiled machine. I was continually typing in their comments, reading them back, and changing them as we polished the wording. When all the changes were agreed upon, the document was finished, and all we had to do was print it, proof it, and sign it. My lawyer said, "That was great."

When I got up to leave, Diane seemed on the verge of tears. In one of my less graceful moments I said, "This is what you wanted." And then I went home.

Later that evening, Diane called me thanked me for how I handled myself during the meeting. I appreciated her gratitude and wondered just how unusual our behavior was. I was also thrilled that God had enabled me to so quickly recover from the driving incident just as He had from the argument at Diane's apartment a few months before. I was beginning to understand that grace shines brightly in the most difficult circumstances.

Job Loss

A few years following our separation, Diane had completed her master's degree and secured a job as a special education teacher. She had been in her new position for less than a year when I received a distressed phone call from her.

Diane told me that she had slipped up one day at work and that the principal and her supervisor were planning to fire her. The more we talked about what happened, the more I felt like the school was overreacting in a big way. But that's neither here nor there. They had Diane in their sights, and she needed help figuring out what to do.

She was really upset. She was told that whether she quit or was fired, she could never work for the school system again. Since it's such a large employer in the area, and Diane worried that potential employers would be suspicious of her exit, she felt like she wouldn't be able to find a job.

I reminded her about the time I was forced out of a company and thought the same thing. I told her things would work out and that I loved her and would welcome her back to our house if she ever hit a rough patch financially. She was so thankful to hear these things.

A few weeks later, in the late afternoon, Diane called me at work and asked if I'd be willing to meet with the head of the teacher's union with her. I said I'd be happy to. Then she clarified that she meant within a half-an-hour. I hopped up, gathered my stuff, and headed out the door.

After I arrived at the meeting, the three of us chatted about the situation, Diane's options, and the pros and cons of each. It seemed clear that she should simply resign and move on. It was also clear that Diane needed support while she worked through this highly charged issue, and she considered me to be an integral part of her team. I felt good about that.

Later that evening, Diane called me to thank me for showing up on short notice and helping her. She made the statement I included at the beginning of this chapter. She said, "The head of the [teacher's] union couldn't believe you're my ex-husband. She hasn't talked to her ex in five years. I told her you do things like this because of the grace of Jesus Christ."

I can't tell you how many times I've heard comments like this. People were noticing the different nature of our relationship, and Jesus was receiving the credit.

The Trial

Not long after Diane's termination ordeal, I had a work-related challenge of my own. On an early November day, the company's CEO popped his head into my office and asked me to join him for a chat. When I walked into his office, one of the company co-founders, who served as the head of human resources, was also there. After we all sat down and exchanged pleasantries, the CEO started talking about the downturn in company revenues. He noted the overhead nature of my role and its associated salary. He then said they had made the difficult decision to let me go.

From that point on, I couldn't really process anything else. My mind was off to the races assessing the impact this would have on my family and me. When the CEO finished speaking, he asked me if I had any questions. I confessed that I didn't catch much after he told me they were letting me go, and that I would need some time to think. They said that was fine.

Then I looked down at my lap and became very emotional. I started choking up and began to thank them for what they had done for me. I told them that they gave me a job at a very difficult time in my life, and that it really saved me. I thanked them several times. This was not your typical reaction to a firing. They were incredibly moved by my words and emotions. Their eyes were filled with tears.

I met the founder's wife the following morning to hand over my laptop and keys and, when we were finished, I thanked her again and gave her a big hug.

At this point, without any income, I needed temporary relief from paying alimony and child support. I could get that in one of two ways. Diane could agree to relieve me, and we would file the paperwork together, or I could seek relief from the courts.

Over the next couple of weeks, I asked Diane a few times if she would give me this relief. She said she would not. While I never asked her why she responded this way, I suspect that she was scared to make any decision that she might later regret. She chose to let the courts do it for her.

Unfortunately, the drumbeat of un-grace reared its ugly head again, and people began saying things like, "After all you've done for her, and she can't give you relief? If I were you I would…." The last sentence always ended with something mean-spirited.

Despite three and a half years of amazing experience with the power of God's grace, I started to buckle a little. It was only when I prayed and asked for guidance that I righted my ship, so to speak. I recommitted to grace and decided to walk through the process accordingly. At that point I had no choice but to take her to court. I called her and explained all the things I was going to do so there would be no surprises. I encouraged her to contact her lawyer, and she informed me that her lawyer had retired, shut down her business, and moved to the Carolinas. I couldn't have been happier with this news, given the beating her attorney had inflicted on me.

I drafted a court order with minimal help from my original attorney and began feeding Diane updates. She responded to none of them. I sent a final update to her the night before the trial and still heard nothing back.

On the day of the hearing, I was outside the courtroom with a large crowd of people who were also there for a hearing. I stood with Diane and her attorney and chatted with them. This was not the norm. All the men were in a seating area on one side of the courtroom entrance, and the women were on the other side.

At one point I looked down the long hallway and saw what I thought was Diane's former attorney. I looked at Diane and said, "Isn't that Alice coming down the hall?" Diane said it couldn't possibly be her since she had left the area. I kept looking at the woman as she came closer and closer and said, "I think that's her."

Soon enough, the woman came all the way down the hall, and it was, in fact, Alice. She saw Diane, and they gave each other a warm hug. Then she saw me and looked at the floor with disdain as she mumbled a greeting in response to my hello.

I had been praying for some time that I would have the opportunity to share our "grace story" with Alice. When Diane said she had moved out of the area, I stopped thinking about it. I figured I would never see Alice again. But here she was, on the same day, in the same building, on the same floor, outside the same courtroom, and at the same time as Diane and me.

I looked at Alice and told her I thought we were meant to see each other that day. I told her that I had an amazing grace story to share with her. Then I gave her a card with a link to a book I had written and posted online that honestly details the things I had done wrong in my marriage.[15] She looked at the card and muttered, "Grace is good." Then she turned away and went to the person she had come to town to help as a favor. The fact that I had given a Web link containing a confession of my wrongdoings to Diane's former attorney—a pit bull of an attorney, to boot—was remarkable. I was psyched.

The rest of the day was challenging. We spent quite a bit of time with mediators trying to hammer out an agreement before our names were called for a hearing. Despite the fact that I offered numerous concessions to get the ball over the goal line, Diane couldn't bring herself to agree with anything. Since there were so many people in court that day, it was three o'clock in the afternoon before we knew it. We had been there for five hours.

We were sitting in a courtroom watching couple after couple fight over the most trivial items as if each one was the end of the world. At one point I looked over at Diane. Her eyebrows were furrowed, and she was picking at her fingers. I realized that the pre-divorce Ed would have been pissed off at her. But all I felt at the time was compassion. I knew this type of thing was not what she was made to do, and it was agonizing for her. It used to be the sort of thing that I would take care of, with a lot of complaining, but now I was actually her opponent.

---

[15] www.just1book.com.

A few minutes later, our names were finally called and Diane, her attorney, and I headed down the hall to another courtroom. Diane's attorney had reached a point of impatience with Diane's hesitance to settle. She was letting her know that as kindly as she could as we made our way.

When we got to the new courtroom, we were the only people there. The judge was summoned, and he came in looking highly irritated. He proceeded to tell us what time it was and that we were "the last people in the building." While that was not technically true, I wasn't about to argue.

He asked if we thought we were close to a settlement. I spoke up and said I thought we were. I said I felt the only issue was that the opposing attorney was trying to make me sign an agreement she brought with her that day despite me sending my own version to them several times in the weeks leading up to the trial. I said I'd really prefer to use my agreement. He looked at the opposing attorney and said, "Do you have a problem with that?"

She suddenly changed her tune and said, "No."

The judge then told us we had fifteen minutes to go out in the hall and finalize the agreement. If we were unsuccessful, he would bring us back in and we would have the trial.

We headed out into the hall and Diane's lawyer immediately started marking up my document. I protested, explaining that I had written the document honestly in the spirit of the original divorce decree, and I asked Diane to vouch for me. In the sweetest voice, Diane told her lawyer that I was correct and to change the document back. I was so proud of her.

We headed back into the courtroom and the judge reappeared. He asked if we had an agreement, and we said, "Yes." As he looked it over, he seemed a little surprised. He looked at me and said, "Do you agree that for every dollar you make you will give your ex-wife 'x' cents in alimony."

I said, "Yes."

Then he said, "Do you realize that for every dollar you make, you will give your ex-wife 'y' cents in child support?"

I said, "Yes." He shook his head in disbelief.

He signed the order and then looked up at me with a beaming smile. He asked me what I did, and I told him that I work in high tech and that I usually find full-time work via consulting opportunities. I explained that this was why the agreement was a little more complex than a typical court order, and that I wanted to make sure that Diane was taken care of.

He looked at me and then Diane, still smiling, and said, "I see a lot of people come through here, and I almost never see anyone like you two. It's really nice to see." I was blown away. I thought I had behaved poorly that day given all the pressure I was under. It was then that I realized that Ed Melick at his worst after the divorce was *way* better than Ed Melick at his best *before* the divorce. This was a profound confirmation of how far I had come.

Diane, her attorney, and I headed out into the hallway. They talked about follow-up work, and I gave the attorney the same card I gave to Alice. Then Diane's lawyer offered to walk Diane out to her car. Diane told her that she was going to walk out with me. And that's what we did, to the surprise of her attorney. When we got to the garage, we hugged each other and both said, "I love you." Then we went to our cars and headed our separate ways.

The Move

About seven years after our separation, Diane decided to move to a new apartment down the street from her first place.

Our relationship had improved steadily since the divorce was finalized, and we were in a good place. We spoke on the phone often, sought and respected each other's opinions on important issues, and proactively helped each other whenever we could. For example, near the end of one particular vacation I took with Shannon, Diane called and offered to stock my refrigerator so we would have food when we got back late at night. She was also at my condo within a couple hours of the flood I experienced with hot food and a pair of helping hands.

The only issue she had with me at the time was her frustration over my lack of income during the years since losing my job. I had spent much of that time caring for my declining parents and working unsuccessfully to build a career in a field that was quite different than the one I had previously worked in. I had not gone on a single date since Diane and I had split, and Diane never dated anyone seriously.

As I already noted, Diane tended to hold onto things and still had pretty much everything she had taken from our house. She had also added a considerable amount of stuff to her holdings since. Her two-bedroom apartment was jammed to the gills, and she was renting two well-stuffed storage units along her hallway. I began urging her to get a jump on packing and clearing out unneeded things well before her scheduled move date. She told me that things were going well each time I asked.

I also told our daughter to make sure she had her room completely packed before she went back to college in Brooklyn. She assured me that she had done this before returning to school.

When the week of the move arrived, I volunteered to help Diane, and she readily accepted. The move was scheduled for the end of the week on Saturday, and I offered to stop by on Monday. When I showed up at her apartment and stepped inside, I was shocked by what I saw. The place looked the same as it always did—jammed with stuff. Hardly a thing had been packed or disposed of.

I experienced a second shock when I looked at my daughter's room and closet. They were also completely jammed with things that had hadn't been sorted or packed. Shannon had only packed a handful of boxes. I immediately texted her and indicated my displeasure with the situation, and she reminded me that her mom used her rather large closet and parts of her room to store things. She said she couldn't touch those things without Diane telling her to stop.

My overall reaction to what I saw was to conclude that there was simply no way we could pack everything in five days. I shared this with Diane, and she told me she had no choice. She had to be out of her apartment by the end of the day on Saturday.

I wanted to say to her, "What have you been doing for the past several months?" She was in between jobs and had more time than usual to start packing. But that's the sort of thing I would have said prior to the divorce. I realized it would be ungraceful and it wouldn't accomplish anything that helped us constructively move forward.

Instead, I told her I was going to focus on Shannon's room and closet and then the kitchen and living room. I asked her to please focus on her bedroom and personal things that only she could address. We started working in earnest with me encouraging her to get rid of as much stuff as possible.

On Wednesday evening, after three long days, I picked up an old backpack of Shannon's and looked inside. What I discovered was pretty gross. There were hundreds, perhaps thousands, of beetle larvae in it.

As Diane and I scurried around trying to dispose of the bag and looking for bugs and larvae nearby, things got tense. At one point Diane snapped at me, and then I said something that escalated the situation. I was standing in the middle of the chaos of her living room and exclaimed, "This wouldn't be a problem if your place wasn't such a giant mess!" More words were said and then I finally did the unconscionable. I called her a hoarder. That seemed to put her completely over the edge and I responded in kind. There was screaming on both sides, and I stormed out of the apartment.

I made my way to my car and sped down the road in a huff. It didn't take long, though, before I felt bad. I knew Diane struggled with organizing and letting things go, and I was heartbroken at the thought of her doing the rest of the work alone.

After meeting a friend and talking to my mom on the phone, I called Diane and apologized for my words and behavior. She did not apologize for her actions. She was still audibly angry. Toward the end of our conversation, I told her I still wanted to help and asked her what she needed from me. Her voice softened noticeably, and she asked if I could come to her place first thing the next morning. I agreed, and that's what I did.

I spent the next few days continuing to help her pack and move. I can't describe how difficult it was. Diane agonized over a whole host of things, which got worse when the movers showed up on Friday and Saturday to help with the packing. The movers also expected a lot more to have been done, and they were persistently pressuring Diane as she struggled to make decisions about getting rid of certain items.

While I took countless trips to the recycling and trash bins, the amount of stuff left over was still unbelievable. When the movers finished removing everything from the apartment and storage units, they had filled a twenty-six-foot truck. One of the Latino workers kept saying in a heavy Spanish accent, "It's too much stuff. It's too much stuff," as he struggled to get the rear doors on the truck closed.

When the movers finally finished it was late and dark, and we went back to the old apartment to collect some stray boxes and cleaning supplies. When we walked in the door and saw the place empty, I suddenly became emotional. I told Diane, "I need a hug," and she came over to me and we enjoyed a long embrace. I told her I loved her, and she responded by saying the same.

Diane had only said *I love you* a few times in seven years, and on those occasions, I got the sense that it had mistakenly slipped out of her mouth. Now she was so happy that the move was over, and with the help I had given her, that she started saying it far more often from that day forward.

9 | Big Cancer

> She had suffered a great deal from many doctors, and over the years she had spent everything she had to pay them, but she had gotten no better. In fact, she had gotten worse.
>
> Mark 5:26

Over the years I have marveled at how the U.S. healthcare system is both wonderful and awful. This contrast really came into focus when Diane was diagnosed with pancreatic cancer.

Not long after her initial CT scan confirmed the presence of a tumor in her pancreas, a gastroenterologist inserted a probe down Diane's throat and placed a small stent in the duct that passes bile from her liver through the pancreas. He also took a biopsy sample of her tumor during the procedure.

To this day, I'm astonished when I think about this procedure and that it was done on an outpatient basis. I wondered how all the technologies used in the operation were developed. Who designs, refines, and produces these small yet critical stents? What equipment was required to safely move down Diane's throat and insert the stent? What kind of training did the doctors and support staff need to pull off such a feat?

Within a month of the procedure, Diane's bilirubin returned to normal levels and her symptoms subsided, including jaundiced skin and a maddening itch. What a wonderful thing! This also enabled Diane to begin chemotherapy. This is where things went south, in my opinion.

As previously noted, Diane began her treatment with a highly toxic chemotherapy regimen known as Folfirinox. They basically began blasting her entire body with four different poisons and a slew of other "medicines" to counter their nasty side effects.

Within two months from the beginning of treatment, the tumor in Diane's pancreas had increased in size by 96 percent, she weighed 93 pounds versus 118 pounds prior to treatment, the cancer had spread to her omentum, and cancer had also appeared near her stomach and pylorus.

All of this "progress" was made at the cost of the laundry list of symptoms listed in the Grim Prognosis chapter: extreme jaw pain, difficulty using her hands, difficulty talking, neuropathy, fatigue, weakness, fever, swelling, breathing issues, diarrhea, and constipation.

To be fair, Diane's chemo was delayed a month while we waited for her bilirubin levels to drop and we investigated an emerging surgical procedure known as irreversible electroporation (IRE). Regardless, the progression of her disease in the face of the pounding the doctors unleashed hardly made sense to me. It was first-hand evidence of what I learned about conventional cancer treatment as I searched for ways to help Diane. My research and findings were an integral part of our journey.

Dysfunctional Culture

A large, dysfunctional cancer culture has formed over many decades that is doing little to truly cure cancer and ease the suffering of those facing it. It is, however, doing lots to sustain the cancer segment of the healthcare industry, which some people have named "Big Cancer." I came to this conclusion as I walked with Diane through her journey and did a good deal of research along the way. Consider the following:

- The amount of money spent in the United States on cancer therapy since the War on Cancer was declared in 1971 is said to be around two *trillion* dollars.[16]

[16] See Dr. Patrick Quillin's presentation at the 2017 The Truth About Cancer conference in Orlando, Florida.

- The U.S. National Institutes of Health alone has spent $800 billion in taxpayer money on cancer research since 1971.[17]
- In 1900, 5 percent of Americans would develop cancer in their lifetimes. Now, it's 40 percent.[18]
- In the United States, the cost of providing cancer care in 2010 was estimated to be $124.57 billion.[19] This is for one single year. The projected annual spend is expected to rise to between $172 and $207 billion by 2020.[20]
- Worldwide, spending on cancer medicines was $107 billion in 2015 and is projected to clear $150 billion by 2020.[21] It's clear that the cost of medicine, primarily chemotherapy, makes up a significant portion of cancer spending.

The consumer cost of cancer drugs continues to skyrocket. The average monthly cost of chemo for a cancer patient is around $10,000, and costs can easily reach $30,000.[22] Wonder drugs like Keytruda, which is far less effective than its advertising would lead you to believe, exceed $150,000 per year.[23] I recently read an article that said a new lymphoma drug from Novartis will cost $475,000 for a one-time treatment![24]

---

[17] Ibid.

[18] Ibid.

[19] *Projections of the Cost of Cancer Care in the United States: 2010–2020*, Angela B. Mariotto et al., Journal of the National Cancer Institute, January 19, 2011. (See https://www.ncbi.nlm.nih.gov/pmc/articles/PMC3107566/)

[20] Ibid.

[21] https://www.cnbc.com/2016/06/02/the-worlds-2015-cancer-drug-bill-107-billion-dollars.html.

[22] https://www.webmd.com/health-insurance/news/20140506/chemo-costs-in-us-driven-higher-by-shift-to-hospital-outpatient-facilities#1.

[23] See https://www.nytimes.com/2017/06/08/health/cancer-drug-keytruda-tumors.html?hpw&rref=health&action=click&pgtype=Homepage&module=well-region®ion=bottom-well&WT.nav=bottom-well&_r=0.

[24] "US approves first cancer drug to use patient's own cells—with $475,000 price tag," Jessica Glenza, *The Guardian*, August 30, 2017.

Diane's first five chemotherapy treatments averaged $20,203 per treatment; and when you add in the $14,695 Neulasta® shot they gave her after she completed each infusion, the average cost of each treatment was $35,898. Let that sink in. Thank God that most of this was paid for by Diane's health insurance provider.

Given the massive amount of spending that's going on, you would expect that we have made significant progress in the battle against cancer. Consider the following:

- Cancer death rates have been rising. According to Clifton Leaf, "Over the past four decades, the crude [U.S.] mortality rate for all the myriad causes of death apart from cancer, considered together, has dropped 24 percent. The same rate for cancer, meanwhile, has climbed 14 percent."[25] The death rate for heart disease alone decreased 47 percent between 1970 and 2010.[26] Furthermore, the number of new cancer cases each year rose 158 percent from 1971 to 2012, a growth rate that is three times the growth rate of the population over the same period of time.[27]
- The true numbers for cancer mortality and the number of new cases per year have been hidden in statistical distortions. For example, there were 62,000 more cancer deaths in the U.S. in 2009 than in 1990, yet the American Cancer Society reported that the death rate actually dropped by 20 percent.[28] Crude death rates, which are typically reported as the number of deaths per 100,000 people, are not what's being reported. Instead, an adjusted measure called simply the "death rate" is reported. This number factors in corrections that are

---

[25] *The Truth In Small Doses*, Clifton Leaf, 2013, Simon & Shuster, Page 38.
[26] Ibid, Page 36-37.
[27] Ibid, Page 77.
[28] Ibid, Page 40-41.

both good and bad—but overall paint a better-than-actual picture. Also, cancer "survival" is considered to be living five years after diagnosis without any regard to whether someone is still afflicted with the disease or how difficult those five years have been.

- Glowing assessments of drug development abound. The statistics counter this optimism. For example, between 1990 and 2002, while the term *breakthrough* appeared in 691 articles, these breakthroughs resulted in only 45 unique drugs, and only twelve of those were shown to even barely extend lives.[29] Most of the progress made against cancer, like the increase in the five-year breast cancer survival rate, has come from early detection, not the wonderful new drugs the pharmaceutical companies keep telling us about. And the deadliest cancers (pancreas, liver, lung, and brain) remain as deadly as they were four decades ago.[30]

It appears we have spent around two trillion dollars to fight cancer, and the fruit of our efforts is a change in mortality that lags all other diseases and a surprisingly small number of new drugs that minimally extend life while introducing serious side effects and risks.

Conflicts of Interest

Not long ago, I spoke with the top executive of a multi-billion-dollar health care provider who acknowledged that oncologists are the only doctors who routinely profit from the medicines they prescribe, and that this could lead to conflicts of interest. I was surprised that he would say such a thing. While the potential for such

[29] Ibid, Page 59-60.
[30] Ibid, Page 52-53.

a conflict is obvious to me, I had never heard an "insider" make such a statement.

If my internist prescribes an antibiotic for me, or my orthopedist prescribes an anti-inflammatory medicine, I go to the pharmacy to fill the prescription and the doctor is no longer part of the equation. He in no way profits from the sale of the drug.

This is not the case with oncologists who purchase chemo drugs from pharmaceutical companies, mark them up, and "deliver" them to patients. This has been called "buy and resell" by some industry insiders.[31] To make matters sketchier, the cost of chemo drugs is astronomical compared to the cost of drugs that other doctors prescribe.

Like many things that go off the rails, this all started for seemingly good reasons. Special care was needed administering these drugs because of their toxicity. As more drugs became available and their costs began to skyrocket, more and more oncologists began operating infusion centers.

Buy and resell contributed to the rapid escalation of cancer treatment costs, so Congress attempted to fix the problem in the 2003 Medicare Modernization Act. Despite alterations in the reimbursement structure, though, doctors still generated significant income when they chose more expensive therapies and applied them more frequently. The new "fee-for-service" model did not fix the problem.

One doctor wrote, "It's difficult, if not impossible, to prove this shift is directly motivated by personal financial gain. But it's also hard to deny the financial gain that resulted."[32] A conflict between the medical interests of a patient and the financial gain of a physician exists.

To make matters worse, hospitals have begun encroaching on these services and recent studies show they are dramatically

---

[31] *Are Oncologists Recommending The Best Treatments For Patients?*, Robert Pearl, M.D., Forbes Magazine, August 7, 2014.
[32] Ibid.

inflating prices.[33] Among the markups found by one study was a $4,500 charge for a dose of irinotecan that typically sells for $60. Clearly, something is wrong with the system.

A Revealing Bible Story

All of this reminds me of a healing account in the Bible about a woman who had suffered from a bleeding problem for many years. One version is recounted in the book of Mark:

> *Jesus went with [Jarius], and all the people followed, crowding around him. A woman in the crowd had suffered for twelve years with constant bleeding. She had suffered a great deal from many doctors, and over the years she had spent everything she had to pay them, but she had gotten no better. In fact, she had gotten worse. She had heard about Jesus, so she came up behind him through the crowd and touched his robe. For she thought to herself, "If I can just touch his robe, I will be healed." Immediately the bleeding stopped, and she could feel in her body that she had been healed of her terrible condition... And [Jesus] said to her, "Daughter, your faith has made you well. Go in peace. Your suffering is over."*[34]

It's telling to note that this woman had spent all her money on doctors who caused a great deal of suffering while her condition worsened. It's amazing that people are still suffering at the hands of some doctors today. Diane's first chemo regimen is proof of that. She experienced lots of suffering, her insurance company spent gobs of money, and she still got sicker.

---

[33] See http://www.charlotteobserver.com/news/special-reports/prognosis-profits/article9083777.html.

[34] Mark 5:24-34.

I suspect that if Diane's oncologist were asked to explain what happened, he would point to the efficacy of her second chemo regimen. He did this often during our office visits while failing to acknowledge the many other things she was doing as well. It's my opinion that these alternative strategies were as important, and in some cases *way* more important, as the treatments she received from him.

What Would Doctors Do?

As I walked alongside Diane on her treatment journey, I wondered what doctors would do in a similar situation. Do they also take highly toxic drugs that show little promise, or do they try something different?

I discovered a 2014 Stanford University study that found that most physicians would forgo aggressive treatments at the end of life despite prescribing the same treatments for their patients facing the same prognosis.[35] The study indicated that 88.3 percent of over 1,800 physicians would not pursue an aggressive treatment. The study also states that, "More than 80 percent of patients say that they wish to avoid hospitalizations and high intensity care at the end-of-life, *but their wishes are often overridden* [emphasis mine]." The study is not restricted to cancer, though, and includes all chronic diseases.[36]

Another study was conducted at the McGill Cancer Center in Montreal, Canada, in the late 1980s and published in 1991.[37] The study looked at a variety of cancers and lists doctors' willingness to undergo chemo and radiation for each one. The responses vary

[35] *Do Unto Others: Doctors' Personal End-of-Life Resuscitation Preferences and Their Attitudes toward Advance Directives*, Vyjeyanthi S. Periyakoil et. al., PLOS ONE Journal, May 28, 2014. See: https://bit.ly/2Dil4i4.

[36] A good article about this phenomenon is *How Doctors Choose to Die*, Ken Murray, The Guardian, February 12, 2012. (See https://www.theguardian.com/society/2012/feb/08/how-doctors-choose-die)

[37] *Oncologists vary in their willingness to undertake anti-cancer therapies*, S.E. Lind et al., British Journal of Cancer, 1991. (See https://www.ncbi.nlm.nih.gov/pmc/articles/PMC1977523/pdf/brjcancer00072-0193.pdf)

greatly by the type of cancer, with 98 percent of the doctors indicating they would undergo chemo for stage IV Hodgkin's disease, but only 8 percent saying they would do so for operable colon cancer. For inoperable pancreatic cancer, only 18 percent of the doctors surveyed said they would either definitely or probably undergo chemotherapy.

These were the only two studies I could find that shed light on what doctors actually do when confronting cancer themselves. I did, though, happen to meet a physician at a pancreatic cancer lobbying event on Capitol Hill in the summer of 2017 who gave me some additional insight.

This doctor was practicing medicine in an area other than oncology when he was diagnosed with stage IV pancreatic cancer in July 2016, the same month as Diane. He told me that he had used a chemo sensitivity test to guide his chemotherapy decisions and it led him to forgo the typical first-line treatment using Folfirinox. Diane asked numerous doctors about the same sort of tests and was rebuffed at every turn.

He then explained that he put together his own treatment regimen that included a less toxic combination of chemotherapy drugs coupled with Plaquenil and intravenous vitamin D. When I asked him if Diane could try such an approach, he said that Plaquenil requires a prescription, which he simply wrote for himself.

Next, he was accepted as a patient by a New York-based oncologist who is well known in pancreatic cancer circles for her novel approach to treating the disease. This same oncologist would later reject Diane as a patient.

Finally, the doctor said that he was unwilling to participate in cancer treatment studies because he didn't want to be placed in a control group that was receiving a placebo. I later watched a video of him speaking at a conference where he urged patients to participate in the same sort of studies that he had rejected. The audience gave him a rousing ovation.

My experience with this doctor was both revealing and upsetting. You can judge for yourself if doctors are applying a dual standard to their patients and themselves.

Conclusions

Big Cancer is broken. The system has failed to develop widespread cures despite the massive amount of money that has been spent to do so. Drug companies and oncologists are making a fortune administering highly toxic treatments, and the industry still clings to a sometimes shameful and embarrassing "standard of care" in the face of overwhelming evidence that it works too infrequently and often does great harm.

I have seen numerous industry videos, pamphlets, and advertisements that include the word "cure" when a true cure for most cancers is nowhere in sight.[38] Such claims are deceptive.

One particular conversation really sticks in my memory. When Diane and I first visited a surgeon, he countered the oncologist's assertion that Diane was "almost certainly" palliative. With lots of bluster and over-confidence, he said he could operate on Diane and boasted about a "revolution" occurring in pancreatic cancer care. Diane cried with hope. One could argue that the doctor gave Diane peace for the following three months while her chemotherapy failed and her cancer progressed. I see it quite differently. If she was indeed so close to being inoperable, then he should have said so and maybe she would have picked a different course of treatment—one far less toxic than the awful first regimen of Folfirinox and maybe one that built up her immune system.

Diane's and my difference of opinion regarding her treatment approach did, though, provide opportunities for me to exercise my grace muscle. Whenever I felt strongly that she should try something different than what she was doing, I told her I had something to say that she may not agree with but that I had to say it because I loved

[38] Check out the video at https://bit.ly/2MDvgWW.

her. I also promised to share my thoughts and then accept whatever she chose to do. She typically decided to continue her own path, and I always went back to the grace that demanded that I love her no matter what.

10 | Strands of Grace

> To be a Christian means to forgive the inexcusable, because God has forgiven the inexcusable in you.
>
> C. S. Lewis
> Author and Theologian

During much of the first three and a half years of my separation/divorce, I shared an office with my company's Director of Sales, Sal D'Itri. I often tell people that Sal had a front row seat to my divorce and everything that was happening in my life and family. At times I felt like he should have pulled out a soft drink and a giant tub of popcorn while listening to me as I regaled him with stories of grief, struggle, and grace. We enjoyed sharing an office together and had a good, easy relationship. We talked often about things that were important to us and the criticality of honoring our higher purposes in life.

Toward the end of my tenure at the company, he would occasionally say, "We should do a radio show together," while we were joking around about various topics. My answer was always the same.

"No way," I would say. "I'll wind up getting on the air and saying something stupid that I'll regret, or cursing, or whatever."

When I was released by the company in the fall of 2011, we kept in touch, but the topic of a radio show didn't come up again until the fall of 2015. Sal called me one day and told me that a local, community media organization had just launched a new low-power radio station and that they were looking for content. He wanted to team up and do a radio program.

My initial reaction was disinterest. I had been through a long period of little income while caring for my declining parents, and I was considering productizing a higher purpose survey I had created. Something like a radio program was the furthest thing from my mind. Sal kept pushing and I suggested that we both go off and pray about it for a week, and then come back together and see how we felt.

A week later we were on the phone again and Sal was as pumped as ever. I didn't really feel any strong urgings one way or another, so I decided to lateral the ball to him. I asked him to take a first cut at the application and then send it to me.

Not long after that I received a completed application from him. It's at this point that I started to get more serious. I read everything he wrote and thought about it in terms of what I felt God had called me to do at that point in my life.

I had shared with Sal several years before some revelations I had one morning. While I was praying it occurred to me that I had become what I've termed a "Grace Machine," i.e., someone who has exercised his/her grace muscle so much that extending grace had become second nature. While I wasn't perfect, I had become a way different person than I was prior to my separation.

I chuckled to myself at the term and then, for some reason, began thinking about churches. I thought, most churches aren't Grace Machines. If they were, they would be places in which people of all types would gather to experience the grace of Jesus Christ. Then I thought about businesses and how much damage they can do to their employees, communities, and the environment. I thought, *There aren't many Grace Machines there, either.*

I began to intentionally pray about this, asking God what He wanted me to do with these ideas. Six months later I was released from our company. It occurred to me that this was the third time in four years that I had prayed very deliberately about something, and God seemed to answer with a punch to the face. The first time was the period leading up to my first church men's retreat, and the second was the period leading up to my separation.

Over the months and years that followed my release, I tried several things I thought God was calling me to do, but I was unable to figure out how to make money with any of them. The good news was that I became increasingly focused on prayer, God's Word, grace, and higher purpose.

I started to realize that the radio program could be an excellent channel for sharing the realness, power, impact, and beauty of God's grace. There seemed to be no doubt that such a message was needed to counter all the negativity, extremism, and un-grace in our culture and media. I decided to dive in.

At the time of this writing, Sal and I have been doing the weekly radio program for nearly three years. The reason our show exists is to, "See to it that no one misses out on God's grace."[39] How we do that is by providing compelling examples of grace in action and a spark to get more people expressing it. We host individuals and organizations that are living by grace, so to speak, and we have them issue calls-to-action for listeners to join in and make our families, workplaces, communities, and world better.

We have talked to over one-hundred-and-thirty people. As we hosted more people, we noticed certain themes repeating themselves. I also noticed how these themes overlapped with my experiences expressing grace to Diane. I call these "strands of grace."

These include concepts like a focus on "the least of these" in society, the importance of identifying and honoring a higher purpose, and a spirit of service, sacrifice, and suffering. Several of these "strands" are particularly relevant to Diane's battle with cancer and my relationship with her.

Getting Close

Many of our guests talk of the importance of getting close to people who are different than you and building lasting relationships

---

[39] Hebrews 12:15, CJB.

with them. I can't think of a better example of this than Daryl Davis. Daryl is an African American musician and author who is on a mission to tear down some of the most extreme barriers between whites and blacks in our country.

Nearly fifty years ago, at the age of ten, Daryl returned to the United States after spending much of his childhood overseas where he attended highly diverse schools for children of U.S. foreign-service employees. Not long after coming home, while he was marching in a parade in a Cub Scout troop, a small group of people started pelting him with bottles and rocks, and he was ushered away by the troop chaperones. When he got home, his parents sat him down and told him about racism. It was the first time in his life that he had heard that term, and it led him to ask a question he has been trying to answer ever since: *How can someone hate me who doesn't even know me?*

Years later, while performing with a band at an all-white truck-stop bar, Daryl was approached by a man during a band break who offered to buy him a drink. Daryl was the only black member in the band. Not long into the conversation, the man and his friend told Daryl that they were members of the KKK. Daryl didn't believe them at first, but soon came to realize they were telling him the truth. The man gave Daryl his card and told him to contact him the next time he would be coming to the bar to play.

They saw each other a few more times at the truck stop, and then fell out of touch when the band stopped playing there. Not long after that, it occurred to Daryl that he had lost a great opportunity to try to answer the question he first posed when he was ten years old. He made up his mind that he was going to seek out KKK members, give them a platform to share their beliefs, and try to answer his question.

That's what Daryl has been doing for nearly forty years. He began to track down KKK members, including Grand Dragons (state leaders) and Imperial Wizards (national leaders), and to form deep friendships with them, often attending their rallies and hanging out at each other's homes. As these Klansmen and Daryl got to know each other, the hatreds and prejudices of the Klansmen began to melt away to such an extent that many of them renounced their beliefs, and about forty of them have given Daryl their robes and hoods for display in a museum he's planning to open. Some of the people who left the Klan were very senior in the organization, including Roger Kelley and Scott Shephard, both former Grand Dragons and Imperial Wizards.

Daryl challenged our audience to take the time to get to know people who are not only different from us, but radically opposed to us. He challenged everyone to, "Walk across the cafeteria and sit down with them and learn about them." And he challenged us to keep that going. He said that ignorance breeds fear, which can breed hatred and eventually lead to destruction.

We have heard many stories like Daryl's about people crossing the lines that divide them from others, like when a Christian lawyer successfully defended a Somali Muslim accused by the U.S. Government of piracy and when a university president slept in a metro station on a frigid February night in order to get a better understanding of what the homeless experience.

The most obvious boundary I have personally crossed is the divide with my wife after she left me. When Diane filed for divorce and moved out, I was offered a lot of mean-spirited advice. People told me I needed to get mean, stop talking to her, and cut off communications between her and my family members. I decided to act counter to that advice and express grace, and I went out of my way to cross, as often as possible, the barrier of separation that Diane had set up between us. I determined that every time I had the opportunity to interact with her I would do so—even when she may only be using me to get something done.

I often tell people that until you extend this type of radical, nonsensical grace, you'll never really "get it." You also won't experience true healing and freedom in these situations until you decide to forgive and love those who have hurt you. I was "loving my enemy" and doing good to her as Christ commands.

Listening

The importance of listening is something that comes up over and over when talking to people about grace. One of our guests, Tim Sample from 72 Africa, a non-profit "waging peace" in difficult areas of Africa, shared a very funny story to drive this point home.

Tim told us about Ernesto Sirolli, who spent seven years working with an Italian non-governmental association (NGO) serving African nations. His first assignment was in Zambia, where the NGO was working to teach the Zambians how to grow food. The NGO got to work in a lush valley near the Zambezi River and planted all sorts of Italian fruits and vegetables. They wondered why the Zambians seemed disinterested in what they were doing and thought to themselves, *Thank God we're here. They obviously need our expertise.*

No sooner did the fruit and vegetables appear when two hundred hippos came up out the Zambezi River and ate everything. The NGO employees were running around saying, "My God, the hippos!"

The Zambians responded by saying, "That's why we don't farm in that valley."

The NGO employees asked why they didn't tell them that and the Zambians responded, "You never asked."

Sirolli points out that the American, English, and French NGOs who were working in Africa at the time also failed miserably, and that he eventually became proud of what the Italians accomplished because they at least fed the hippos. The other NGOs didn't even do that.

Sirolli often quotes from the book entitled *Dead Aid,* written by a female Zambian economist named Dambisa Moyo. In it, Moyo notes that western countries spent two *trillion* dollars trying to help Africans over a fifty-year period ending in 2009. She describes the enormous damage the money has done from the perspective of an African woman. Sirolli attributes this to the patronizing attitude of westerners who swoop in like white knights, think they know everything, and treat the locals as less than them.

Sirolli gave a great deal of thought to his own experiences and what he read in *Dead Aid,* and he began to formulate an approach he called Enterprise Facilitation. A central tenant to this approach is that one should never initiate anything but instead become a servant of the passions of local people to help them improve their lives. It involves shutting up, never arriving with pre-conceived notions, meeting with local people in their local settings, and listening to them. It means becoming their friends.

When he first started doing this, he simply walked the streets of a village in Western Australia and started talking to people. Within three days he had his first client, a fisherman whom he helped sell fish to local restaurants. Soon other fisherman came to him, and he helped them sell their fish to Japan for ten times more money than they got locally.

Before long he was helping twenty-seven businesses and the government came to him and asked him how he was doing it. He said, "I'm doing something really difficult. I'm shutting up and listening." They asked him to do more, and today he is working in 300 communities around the world and has helped launch 40,000 businesses.

Tim Sample and his partners at 72 Africa have used this focus on listening to implement several successful peace-making initiatives in Ghana and other areas on the African continent. Listening was also woven into numerous other stories we heard. Whether it's a multi-faith, multi-ethnic advocacy group that schedules listening sessions to identify local community problems, a blind radio host who produces a program that allows disabled people's voices to be heard, or a college professor taking the time to meet with her students one-on-one to carefully listen to them as they describe their passions, talents, and frustrations, the importance of listening keeps coming up.

Sally O'Dwyer from Catholic Charities in Arlington, Virginia, summed it up nicely when she said, "We really underestimate the power of just listening and being there for somebody. People need to be heard, recognized, and reminded that they are a child of God, they have value, and that they matter." Another guest named Joanie Coolidge from Ignatian Volunteer Corps beautifully described what she does as "holy listening."

I applied this approach to my relationship with Diane. A few nights after Diane told me she wanted a divorce, I found myself talking to her as she prepared for bed while our daughter was sleeping. For the first time in ages, I simply shut up and let her talk while I listened intently. I was amazed at the things she said and how broken and hurt she had become. At one point she said, "All I want is for someone to look into my eyes and tell me they love me." This nearly ripped my heart out, and I committed to practice intentional listening from that point on.

Over the years since our separation, I also decided to become a servant of Diane's passions. I supported whatever work and school decisions she made and tried to identify areas where I could help her in any way. One beautiful summer evening, while Diane, Shannon, and I were eating outdoors at one of our favorite restaurants, Diane was lamenting how difficult it was for her to choose and buy a laptop. Toward the end of the meal, I happily slapped the table and said, "We're going to go to the Apple store tonight to help you configure and buy what you need."

Diane immediately responded by saying, "No one else has offered to help me with this."

The three of us headed to the store, Shannon and I helped her configure a machine, and she picked it up the next day. Diane was so thankful. By genuinely listening to her and helping her to do the things that were important to her, I was able to slowly earn back her trust.

This all reminds me of a scripture in the Bible that says everyone should be "quick to listen [and] slow to speak."[40] We would all do well to follow this advice.

Forgiveness

"This man's grandson killed this man's son." This is how Azim Khamisa is often introduced when he appears before groups gathered to hear him speak. His life changed dramatically back in 1995 when his only son, Tariq, was shot and killed while delivering pizzas in San Diego. His killer, Tony Hicks, became the first fourteen-year-old to stand trial as an adult in the state of California. Tony received a twenty-five-year-to-life prison sentence.

Not long after Tariq's death, Azim, a Sufi Muslim, felt compelled to forgive his son's killer. He asked the District Attorney to introduce him to Tony's grandfather, Plez Felix, who was raising him. They eventually met in the public defender's office.

Azim told Plez that he was not there for revenge. He said they had both lost a son, one to murder and another to the criminal justice system. He invited Plez to join him to stop kids from killing kids.

Plez, a southern Baptist, told Azim that he went into his prayer closet when he heard about Tariq's murder and prayed that he would meet Azim so he could extend his deepest condolences to him and his family. He couldn't thank Azim enough for reaching out to him and said that he would be glad to support Azim's efforts to stem violence. Since then, the two men have found themselves sitting side-by-side, shoulders touching, on many stages.

Azim went on to establish the Tariq Khamisa Foundation, an organization committed to stopping children from killing children by breaking the cycle of youth violence. He has written four books, including the trilogy *Murder to Forgiveness*, *From Forgiveness to Fulfillment*, and *Fulfilment to Peace* (in which Tony wrote the forward). He has given over one thousand presentations to over one

---

[40] James 1:19.

million kids worldwide. He has also forgiven Tony, lobbies for his release from prison, and plans to hire him at the Tariq Khamisa Foundation when he's paroled.

Among the many nuggets of wisdom that Azim shared with us is that forgiving leads to peace. He said he has personally experienced a level of peace by forgiving Tony that he could never have imagined. Azim said that judgment is the biggest impediment to forgiveness, and he decided to leave judgment to a higher power. There's no quality of life in being a victim.

He noted that his future daughter-in-law (Tariq's fiancé, Jennifer) was the only person in their family who could not forgive Tony, and she was angry with Azim and others for doing so. She eventually became addicted to drugs and took her own life seven years after Tariq's death. The trajectory of Azim and Jennifer's lives following Tariq's death is powerful evidence that forgiveness is the only way to go.

One of our guests likened un-forgiveness to a disease that will make and keep you sick. The Reverend Dr. Michael Barry served as the Director of Pastoral care at the Cancer Treatment Centers of America in Philadelphia for over ten years. He has spent lots of time with people who are facing death and has learned a great deal about the role of forgiveness in healing physical and emotional illness. He has written about this in a book entitled, *The Forgiveness Project: The Startling Discovery of How to Overcome Cancer, Find Health, and Achieve Peace.*

Dr. Barry notes that finding the motivation to forgive is the number one barrier to forgiveness. He points out that all religions value forgiveness, but the Christian religion *requires* it. The Apostle Paul wrote, "Make allowance for each other's faults, and forgive anyone who offends you. Remember, the Lord forgave you, so you must forgive others."[41] Jesus said we should pray to God to, "forgive

---

[41] Colossians 3:13.

us our sins, as we have forgiven those who sin against us."[42] He also said that, "[If] you forgive other people when they sin against you, your heavenly Father will also forgive you. But if you refuse to forgive others, your Father will not forgive your sins."[43] In a related passage, Jesus said, "I tell you, love your enemies and pray for those who persecute you… Be perfect, therefore, as your heavenly Father is perfect."[44]

Radically loving your enemies, which includes forgiveness, makes you perfect like God is perfect. That's an amazing statement.

Dr. Barry urges people who have cancer to become students of forgiveness. He says it not only helps us learn to cope, but also puts us in touch with the God who loves and forgives us.

Forgiveness is admittedly hard, though. It always hurts, and the greater the wrong the greater the pain. It always costs something to forgive.

Over the past ten years, a key to my ability to forgive Diane and others has been the growing realization of how much I need to be forgiven myself. The more I realized how much I screwed up in my marriage and other relationships, the more willing I was to extend grace and forgiveness to others. In the words of C. S. Lewis, "To be a Christian means to forgive the inexcusable, because God has forgiven the inexcusable in you."[45] My increasing awareness of how flawed I am opened the door to unimaginable grace in my life. It was only when I realized and focused on *my* mistakes and sin that I began to yearn to serve Diane and others and extend grace and forgiveness no matter what.

One of our radio program guests put it this way: "Who can make the case that we have acted unselfishly all of our lives? We are all in need of forgiveness and grace. Karma is real, and Jesus took our

---

[42] Matthew 6:12.
[43] Matthew 6:14-15.
[44] Matthew 5:44,48.
[45] C. S. Lewis, "On Forgiveness," in *The Weight of Glory and Other Addresses*, New York, NY: Collier Books/Macmillan, 1980, pg. 125.

bad karma on himself."[46] Knowing that we've been so graciously forgiven should motivate us to extend the same forgiveness to others.

A Word About Un-grace

These stories and many others like them prove that there is an amazing diversity of grace all around us. Unfortunately, you might not know it by watching the news and browsing the Internet.

Way too often during the early years of my separation and divorce, I was often greeted by someone encouraging me to behave ungracefully. Most of the people I talked to had advice for how to handle my wife and the divorce—and it was often spiteful. In the world, every bad act seems to deserve an equal or greater bad reaction. Many people got mad at me or expressed frustration with me for treating my wife with grace after she left. Yet the wonderful things that came from my decision now stand as a testament to grace. Only one person later came to me and acknowledged that his advice was wrong. Just one person.

Many more, though, have marveled at the relationship I developed with Diane. Marveling is evidently easier than apologizing. I often wondered what my neighbors thought when they saw Diane and me occasionally giving each other a tender goodbye hug in our driveway when she stopped by my house for something. I hope that grace was touching their hearts.

The Bible's concept of grace is not only unique to Christianity, but I believe it's the only force powerful enough to overcome the spirit of un-grace that is so prevalent in the world. This amazing grace is Christianity's greatest contribution to the world and dispensing it should be our highest priority. The good news of grace is that God loves us deeply, and He radically displayed that love through the sacrifice of Jesus Christ. We are called to extend this same grace.

---

[46] Jason Hershey during his October 26, 2016 interview.

11 | Non-Standard Care

> Radical remission cases may not be explainable at the moment, but they are *true*.
>
> Kelly Turner
> Author, Researcher, and Counselor

A little over ten years ago, a young counselor named Kelly Turner was working with cancer patients when she first encountered what she calls "radical remission." She defines radical remission as a case in which a person's cancer goes away without the use of conventional treatment, or through the use of alternative treatments after the failure of conventional treatment, or through a combination of both types of treatments in the face of a dire prognosis.[47]

Turner began searching for other such cases and, to her surprise, found over a thousand in medical journals. Her disbelief was increasingly mixed with frustration, though, as she realized that conventional doctors were not interested in learning more about what these patients had done to get better. Turner soon decided to dedicate her life to finding, analyzing, and sharing such stories.

In 2014, Turner published a book entitled *Radical Remission: Surviving Cancer Against All Odds*. In it, she describes how she traveled extensively, conducting over one hundred in-person interviews and analyzing over one thousand published cases of radical remission. She identified seventy-five factors that potentially played a role in healing and reduced that list to nine key factors that were mentioned far more than the others. Kelly wrote, "...the

---

[47] *Radical Remission, Surviving Cancer Against All Odds*, Kelly A. Turner, 2014, Harper Collins.

majority of Radical Remission cancer survivors I study did all nine of these factors, at least to some degree."[48]

The nine key factors involved patients radically changing their diets, taking control of their health, following their intuition, using herbs and supplements, releasing suppressed emotions, increasing positive emotions, embracing social support, deepening their spiritual connections, and having a strong reason for living.[49]

For me, the most fascinating thing about this list is that only two of the nine factors are physical: nutrition and supplements. The remainder of the list involves emotional, cognitive, and spiritual factors.

As if anticipating the typical arguments of Western doctors when confronted with such evidence, Kelly writes, "Radical Remission cases may not be explainable—at the moment—but they are *true*."[50]

Integrated Beings

Human beings are an absolute marvel in their complexity and function. This perspective was captured beautifully by King David thousands of years ago when he wrote that we are "fearfully and wonderfully made." The Hebrew words that David used to describe man and God's creativity in Psalm 139 indicate something that should astonish us, something that is extraordinarily difficult to design, create, and understand.

When you consider the many organs and systems that manage, regulate, and sustain each of us, it's awe-inspiring. Organs such as the eye, brain, and heart are amazing in their design, function, complexity, and elegance. There are also many systems that govern

---

[48] Ibid, page 9.

[49] It's worth noting that exercise is not on the list. This came as a surprise to me. Kelly addressed this by noting that most people are too sick to exercise when they begin their healing journey, and that "almost all of them eventually exercise regularly." She acknowledges that movement and exercise are essential to good health.

[50] *Radical Remission, Surviving Cancer Against All Odds*, Kelly A. Turner, 2014, Harper Collins, page 10.

the proper functioning of a human being, including the cardiovascular, pulmonary, neuromuscular, cognitive, emotional, limbic, endocrine, and adrenal systems. Some systems are even specialized, such as the endocannabinoid system that regulates a host of physiological and cognitive processes as it mediates the effects of marijuana on a person. These all work together in wonderful harmony to sustain life and enable the functionality we sometimes take for granted.

An ever-increasing number of scientists, researchers, and doctors realize that, in order to properly care for ourselves and promote healing when we are sick, we need to consider all these systems and organs as an integrated whole. By caring for the whole person, we can improve health, prevent disease, and better treat illness.

This is not the approach of traditional medicine, which focuses far too often on disease management rather than prevention and healing. This is particularly true for serious chronic conditions like cancer, diabetes, and Alzheimer's. As more and more people become frustrated with traditional medicine's shortcomings in the treatment of these conditions, they are looking at alternative approaches to health, wellness, and healing.

There are a number of terms used to describe treatments and care that lie outside the boundaries of conventional medicine. Examples include alternative medicine, complimentary medicine, integrative medicine, holistic medicine, functional medicine, unconventional care, and non-standard care.

Definitions of these terms can be very unflattering. For example, Wikipedia defines alternative medicine as "practices claimed to have the healing effects of medicine but which are disproven, unproven, impossible to prove, or are excessively harmful in relation to their effect; and where the scientific consensus is that the therapy does not, or cannot, work because the known laws of nature are violated by its basic claims; or where it is considered so much worse than conventional treatment that it would be unethical to offer as treatment."[51] The Wikipedia definition also includes links to topics like quackery, pseudoscience, and pseudo medicine. Clearly, the person who wrote this is not a fan of alternative medicine.

As I've stated, during Diane's illness, I focused on the topic of alternative medicine. I accompanied Diane on nearly all her doctor visits and no one we met suggested that Diane try anything outside of the "standard of care." No one reacted favorably when we mentioned things like better nutrition, supplements, or non-toxic therapies that lie outside the control of Big Pharma. This is disappointing considering the mounting evidence indicating the profound effect that things like diet, herbs, and even fasting have on our ability to prevent, slow down, halt, and, potentially, cure disease.

As I investigated non-standard approaches to disease prevention and treatment, there were a handful of factors I came across repeatedly. Several of these are found in Kelly Turner's list above, like good nutrition, spiritual practices, and the importance of releasing negative emotions and holding onto positive ones. Others include things like sleep, eliminating toxins, non-sleeping rest, stress management, and exercise.

It's becoming generally accepted that we should eat a diet that consists primarily of vegetables, fruit, seeds and nuts; minimize or eliminate our intake of sugar, white flour, and processed foods; consume high-quality animal proteins in moderation; exercise and generally move more throughout each day; sleep seven-to-eight hours per night; rest/recharge during waking hours through meditation, relaxation, hobbies and fun; avoid toxins like tobacco, illicit drugs, and environmental pollutants; and minimize and eliminate stress and negative/unhealthy attitudes and beliefs.

When I read this list, I wonder who could possibly do all these things. As an example, Diane was excellent at getting exercise, but

[51] November 14, 2017 definition.

she struggled mightily to get the proper amount of sleep every night, and nothing she tried helped her resolve this problem. For at least fifteen years, she resisted going to bed at a reasonable time, often sleeping between two and four hours per night, and she showed up to numerous chemotherapy sessions after staying up the entire night before. It's difficult to prevent illness or to heal when you are chronically tired. Most people are like this, thriving in some areas while falling short in others.

I also came across several cancer therapies that face significant or insurmountable obstacles, such as the lack of FDA approval or no health insurance coverage. Examples of these include things like cannabis, Laetrile, and Antineoplastons. When we mentioned these treatment approaches to mainstream doctors, we were typically met with either indifference or skepticism. Regardless, I began to collect information on these approaches to consider in the event that Diane's cancer began spreading again or her chemo became intolerable.

Mainstream treatment providers are quick to say that non-standard approaches lack scientific evidence. A counter argument can be made that numerous players in the cancer industry have been working to limit funding and support for such studies. Even worse is the fact that mainstream medicine's own studies of standard treatment protocols frequently show abysmal results. Conventional medicine may be provable, but it's too often provably awful.

How did we get here?

While an increasing number of doctors are suggesting methods such as acupuncture and support groups as a means of helping patients deal with cancer, the notion of turning to factors such as nutrition or therapies outside of Big Pharma's control is unthinkable. The question is, *Why?*

One interesting explanation for this comes from a gentleman named G. Edward Griffin who wrote the book *World Without*

Cancer. Griffin says that the topic of curing cancer can be summed up in the following thirty-five words: A control for cancer is known and it comes from nature, but it is not widely available to the public because it cannot be patented and therefore is not commercially attractive to the pharmaceutical industry.[52]

The move toward Big Pharma's dominance of the U.S. medical sector began when foundations created by Andrew Carnegie and John D. Rockefeller began to exert influence on the look and operation of the industry.

At the start of the 20th century, the Carnegie Foundation for the Advancement of Teaching commissioned a series of studies of various segments of the U.S. higher education system. One of these studies resulted in the *Flexner Report*, a comprehensive evaluation and report on the state of U.S. medical education. The report summarized the then-current state of affairs, proposed a vision of the characteristics of ideal schools, and provided assessments, typically harsh, of each medical school in the U.S. and Canada.

In 1913, Abraham Flexner, who spearheaded the research and development of his namesake report, was hired by John D. Rockefeller's General Education Board (GEB) to utilize its resources to bring about the changes that Flexner proposed. With $45 million in grant money (worth over a billion dollars today), the GEB started funding select universities, and later, public schools, who were friendly to their philosophy of how medical education should be delivered. They also placed foundation members on the boards of directors at these institutions. Over the years, these schools began to reflect the agenda and priorities of Rockefeller, Carnegie, their business interests, and the people chosen by them. The medical industry naturally followed.

According to Edward Griffin, their agenda was, "to improve their public image through the appearance of philanthropy; to

[52] *The Politics of Cancer* presentation given by Edward Griffin at the 2017 Truth About Cancer Presentation in Orlando Florida.

preserve their fortunes from income and inheritance taxes by concentrating them in tax foundations that they controlled; and to *finance commercially profitable or ideologically desirable projects* [emphasis mine] through philanthropy." [53]

Griffin considered it a brilliant strategy. While the technical quality of medical education was indeed elevated, the curriculum and staff at schools became predominantly oriented toward drug therapies that Rockefeller and Carnegie businesses wanted to sell to them. Today, doctors get no training in things like nutrition because that's not where the money is. Mr. Griffin says that doctors have, to a large degree, been converted into salesmen for the pharma industry. Writing prescriptions is what they've been trained to do.

Differing Attitudes

I experienced first-hand the difference in attitude between conventional medicine and non-standard treatment providers when I filled out two forms with Diane.

The first form was given to us by the expert in botanical medicine who formulated the regime of supplements that Diane began taking in February 2017. I was impressed with the completeness of information being collected. He wanted to know *everything* about Diane's medical history and the things she had tried to combat her cancer. Besides the standard stuff, like current medications and family medical history, he asked for information on a host of other topics. These included every modality of treatment Diane has ever used and/or was currently using and her frequency of use; how she felt about her relationships, diet, exercise, finances, spirituality, and a host of other aspects of her life; and a summary of everything she put in her mouth over a recent three-day period. He even asked her to write a cancer narrative, a cancer self-portrait, and a healing portrait. I thought this was great. This man was truly interested in developing a complete picture of Diane's life and

[53] Ibid.

cancer journey. It reminded me of the expression, "Everything counts."

The second form was Web-based and is used by a nonprofit organization to collect treatment information from pancreatic cancer patients. I helped Diane fill this form out in the summer of 2017. The form asks a lot of questions about surgery, radiation, and chemotherapy treatments. Then it asks if there are other things the patient has tried. If you hit *yes*, a tiny input box opens. One small box.

The contrast between the two forms was striking. Diane noted that the second form could give the impression that all the progress she had made fighting her disease is due solely to chemotherapy treatments. She had been complementing her chemo with a host of physical, emotional, and spiritual therapies which we believed had a profound effect on her health. To ignore these seemed to be narrow-minded.

Diane's Approach

As the end of 2018 approached, Diane had a pretty good quality of life considering the severity of her disease, her chemo treatments, and their side effects. She had lived longer than we had expected, and we were thankful.

Diane's improvement occurred just as she stopped her highly toxic first-line chemotherapy and began implementing a host of non-standard treatments to build up her immune system:

- Diane grew increasingly closer to and more reliant on God. After attending only three church services over the first eight years of our separation, she began attending every Sunday that she was physically able to and would listen to online sermons when she couldn't. She attended "a church for people who don't go to church,"[54] which offered her a safe and welcoming environment where she could renew her relationship with God.

- Diane met with people involved in healing ministries.
- I consistently sent updates on Diane's health to a steadily growing list of people and asked them to pray for Diane. I'm fairly certain that several hundred people have interceded with God on Diane's behalf.
- Our family deliberately shifted to a more hopeful/positive frame of mind than the vibe of death and glumness we were getting from the doctors.
- Our daughter came home from school in December 2016 and moved in with Diane. I don't think anyone can underestimate the positive impact of this.
- Diane slowed down significantly: partly out of necessity, like when she had to stop working, and partly by choice, like taking time to have leisurely meals with Shannon and me.
- Diane, Shannon, and I spent a good deal of time together as a family.
- Diane reconnected with her closest sorority sisters who offered her a great deal of support, companionship, and love.
- Diane received emotional and other support from many cancer-related groups including a cancer counselor, a Life with Cancer small group, and people she met through the Pancreatic Cancer Action Network.
- Diane had been on an extensive regimen of botanicals and other supplements for ten months. The protocol included things we were familiar with (vitamins B, C, D, and K), things we knew a little about (curcumin,

[54] This is the tagline for Grace Community Church in Arlington, VA (See www.trygrace.org).

mistletoe, and ginger), and herbs we had never heard of (Ligustrum, Japanese knotweed, and astragalus).
- She was doing more fun things than she had prior to her diagnosis, including taking trips and going to concerts.
- She began working out again. Of course, she was limited in what she could do, but it meant the world to her to get to the gym and see her buddies.
- Diane tried other forms of care, including acupuncture, meditation, and chiropractic treatment.

There's a lot going on in this list. I can imagine that any combination of these things could have contributed to Diane's improved condition. There are also important things that are absent from the list, like quality sleep and a radical change in diet. These were things that Diane was either unable or unwilling to change. Most important, though, is that Diane and I moved from a state of sadness, fear, and worry to a state of confidence in God's power to heal her and to richly bless her whether He did so or not.

Conclusions

I have never met anyone who lived five years or more with an advanced form of cancer using only non-standard treatments. I have read stories and seen videos about such people, but it's not a common occurrence. I believe there are several reasons for this.

Mainstream medicine is massive and growing. Healthcare spending in the U.S. alone was $3.5 *trillion* dollars in 2017, which represents 17.9 percent of our country's Gross Domestic Product.[55] It's difficult to shift the inertia of such a behemoth from symptom management to a prevention and wellness model.

The greed of industry players is causing untold suffering. You don't have to look hard to find stories of drug companies earning

[55] Centers for Medicaid and Medicare Services (www.cms.org), National Health Expenditure Data.

handsome profits while pushing drugs that are highly toxic or addictive or raising prices for lifesaving drugs to the point where people can't afford them.[56] Furthermore, there are many examples of industry players working to discredit and suppress promising, inexpensive treatment options.[57]

The typical western diet is both addictive and terrible for our health. Refined sugar can be found in nearly all processed foods and genetically modified foods abound. Furthermore, it's expensive to eat healthy, especially if you choose only organic foods, and it takes hard work to avoid foods with unhealthy ingredients. In addition, we are being bombarded with toxins. We probably can't even imagine the toll that the thousands of man-made chemicals in our environment are having on us. Cost is a factor, as well. Non-standard care is almost always *not* covered by health insurance. Finally, people get scared when suddenly confronted with a serious illness, and they often turn to treatments that are considered mainstream and "trustworthy."

In Diane's case, she considered non-standard treatments only after it became clear that her first line of chemotherapy was failing, and she had suffered a great deal from its side effects. Even then, though, she embarked on a new regimen of chemo just as she was diving into non-standard care. She, like so many, was unable to completely shake her fear of the unknown and continued favoring the traditional.

---

[56] For just a few of many examples, check out Purdue Pharma, Oxycontin producers who have made a fortune aggressively pushing the sale of their highly addictive drugs; Turing Pharmaceuticals, whose founder raised the price of a drug used mainly to treat a rare infection in babies and HIV patients by 5,000 percent; and GlaxoSmithKline, who paid $7.9 billion in 31 settlements over a 24-year period.

[57] Watch the *Second Opinion: Laetrile at Sloan-Kettering* documentary for an example.

12 | Spreading Grace

> I talk about you often and the influence you have had, and your story.
>
> Excerpt from a note from a divorced man to me
> 2014

Not long after our divorce was finalized, I decided to start extending the same level of grace to others that I had shown to Diane.

I began with my parents, who were advanced enough in age and sufficiently frail that neither one of them could drive. I decided I would visit them every weekend to take my dad grocery shopping and visit my mom afterwards. I also decided that I would try to take them to as many of their doctor's appointments as possible. They lived about twenty minutes from my house, so I figured it wouldn't be that hard. I was wrong.

The doctor visits alone turned out to be a huge undertaking given their many health problems. I soon discovered that a single ailment might require six or more visits to doctors, labs, and imaging centers, and some of those visits stretched out for three or four hours.

Between work, managing my house and personal affairs, and helping my parents, it got a little crazy. There were many Saturdays that I sat exhausted on my parents' couch after creeping slowly around the grocery store with my disabled dad and then visiting with and helping my mom.

My parents' reaction made it all worth it, though. On numerous occasions when I was leaving after a visit, my dad would take my hand and kiss it and thank me profusely. My mom was also super thankful.

Following one doctor's appointment where my dad was told he likely had hydrocephalus on top of his many other health problems, I asked him if he'd like me to pray for him and my mom. We were standing in their kitchen. Dad had long been an avowed atheist, and my overly legalistic behavior during the early days of my faith had done nothing to attract him to Christ. This would be the first time in my life that I had prayed with him. He surprisingly agreed.

During the prayer, I wept as I thanked God for my parents and all they had done for me in my life. I asked God to compress both of their morbidities as they aged and moved toward death and I shared the Gospel. I thanked God for His coming kingdom where there would be no more blindness, deafness, or lameness—all conditions that Dad suffered from to one degree or another.

After the prayer, my dad looked up, bear-hugged me, and said, "You're not just a great son; you're the best." I had imagined any number of responses besides this one, and I was overjoyed at his unrestrained expression of thankfulness and joy and that God was encouraging me to boldly share the Gospel of hope with him.

I would go on to pray numerous times with Dad and Mom following doctor visits. He was always appreciative and would say things like, "What a nice prayer!" and "Thank you so much for that." My mom would later tell me how much he liked and appreciated those prayers. One thing that really touched me deeply was that whenever I would say, "Let's pray," he would quickly close his eyes and put his hands together like a child. This reminded me of when Christ said that we must have faith like little children.

On the next-to-last Thanksgiving that I spent with my mom and dad, my dad grabbed my arm following a prayer and said he agreed with everything I had said, including the Gospel. I was thrilled to hear this.

The following October, Dad fell in the garage of his building and was taken to the hospital. The doctors soon discovered that he had experienced a mild heart attack that had caused him to lose consciousness and fall. One night, before a risky procedure he was scheduled to undergo early the next morning—a procedure we weren't sure he would survive—I said a very emotional prayer with my parents. I emphasized the Gospel as always. When I finished, Dad said, "You're the best thing to happen to me in my life." I'm convinced that Dad was reacting to the power of the Gospel, not anything I had done. As the apostle Paul wrote to the Romans, "For I am not ashamed of this Good News about Christ. It is the power of God at work, saving everyone who believes."[58] It was certainly the power of God at work in this case.

It occurred to me that Dad was far more open to the Gospel when he was in need and I was willing to help him with no strings attached. When I was legalistic and selfish years before, it pushed him away. When I sacrificially served him without wavering or complaining, he was all ears.

Dad fell again at the start of the following year and broke his hip. He passed away after nine weeks of hospital and rehabilitation center stays. His loss was difficult, but I am greatly comforted that I will see him again because of the power of grace.

Grace at Work

I began looking for opportunities to express grace at work as well. A good example involved a young female co-worker named Tina. One day I noticed Tina moving about the office with a somewhat downcast look on her face. As the day progressed, her countenance didn't improve, so I eventually asked her to join me in my office. I asked her why she looked so down. She started talking about the difficulties she faced working in the U.S. as a green card holder, struggling with the English language, and missing her family back home.

When she finished sharing, I tried to encourage her. I told her she had the world by the tail, so to speak, given her master's degree, specialized work experience, and her growing fluency in English. I

[58] Romans 1:16.

shared that she was well-respected at work and that she should be heartened by that, and I invited her to chat with me whenever she needed help, advice, or more encouragement. She thanked me for my comments and went back to work. Over the next several days, Tina looked far different—positive and energized. She eventually came to me and thanked me for pulling her aside. She said I was the only person to notice she was struggling and to ask her what was wrong.

Tina and I began chatting more frequently and enjoyed joking around in the office. At one point she asked me to help her update her resume, and we agreed to have a working session at a nearby Panera Bread one day after work. We sat outside that evening, enjoying a beautiful summer day while we made real-time improvements to her *curriculum vitae* (CV) on my laptop.

About three years into our relationship, I told Tina about a local conference where a Christian missionary who had lived in numerous Muslim countries would be speaking. Tina grew up in a predominantly Muslim nation, and I thought she would enjoy hearing about his experiences. When I told her about the event, she was pleasant but noncommittal. Since Tina was in her twenties and single, and the conference was on a Friday night, I didn't have much hope that she would show up.

When the night of the event rolled around, I found myself in the far suburbs of Washington, D.C., at a church that looked more like a data center than a house of worship. I wasn't even thinking about Tina as I chatted with a group of attendees around a large, round table. At one point I felt a tap on my shoulder. I turned and there was Tina. I was excited to see her. We chatted a bit and I asked her where she would like to sit for the presentations. She said she wanted to sit somewhere up front.

There were four speakers that night, with the last one being the person I most wanted her to hear. Tina heard the Gospel that night, perhaps for the first time, and she saw Christians interacting with Muslims in a way that was quite surprising to her. Each speaker emphasized the importance of modeling Jesus' example when working in other nations, and they told story after story of the impact they had extending radical grace to Muslims. Following the presentations, Tina wanted to chat with the featured speaker. She went up to him and told him that she had never heard a Christian speak the way he had spoken. She seemed moved and encouraged by everything she heard. The next day Tina returned for the morning session, and she brought her brother with her, who was in the U.S. for a few weeks to visit her.

I don't think Tina would have heard the Good News she heard that night if I had not noticed her a few years before and taken the time to engage, listen to, and encourage her.

Six months later, when I was released from the company where we both worked, I left a gift-wrapped Bible and note on Tina's desk. She called me later that day when she heard the news and insisted on meeting for dinner. We picked my favorite restaurant and she surprised me with two boxes of my favorite cookies from Trader Joe's. It was clear that she valued my friendship and was sorry to see me suddenly get released.

Tina and I continue to be friends in the seven years since I left that company. While I don't believe she has been born again, I trust that she's on her own journey, safe in the plan Christ has for her. My job is to keep extending grace to her no matter what that journey looks like.

Grace Across the Country

An interesting thing happened as my experience with grace grew and more people heard about my divorce. I started getting phone calls and e-mails from people looking for help in the D.C. Metro area and beyond.

One example is a man named Allen who lives in California. Allen emailed one day in late winter 2012, at the suggestion of a mutual friend, Derrick, who attended my church. Here's a portion of his note:

> *My wife and I are divorcing after 11 1/2 years of marriage. I have known her since I was 16, high school sweethearts. This is where I met Derrick, also at age 16. Derrick has known my wife since he was 10. That was why it was such a shock in November when I found out she had been having an affair with a woman. She told me she was gay and wanted out of our marriage.*
>
> *Obviously, my world has been rocked. Derrick was the first person I reached out to and he put me in touch with one of his friends who knew about being in the desert in total brokenness.*
>
> *Derrick [also] sent me the link to your online book, [and] he said you wanted me to contact you. So here I am. I would be open to whatever you have [for] me and I would appreciate any of your time. Thanks.*

Not long after receiving Allen's note, we had a long phone conversation. Among many things, he noted that he and his wife had two daughters, ages three and six, and he was very concerned about what a divorce would do to them. At the tail end of our talk, I shared my story with Allen and told him that grace, radical Christ-like grace, was his only real option for dealing with the situation. He didn't seem convinced.

Months later, I got an excited phone call from him. He informed me that he had thought I was nuts following our first conversation, but after hitting an emotional low about two months after we spoke, he had decided to take my advice to heart. He said he began to treat his wife gracefully whenever they interacted, especially when they exchanged their daughters at the end of each week. He said he was encouraged about the effect it had had on their relationship.

Then Mother's Day arrived, and he became angry. He wondered how he could wish her happy Mother's Day after all *she* [emphasis mine] had done to their family. He said he prayed for God's strength to continue with grace. When he saw her later that day, he felt something come over him, and he gently put his hand on her shoulder and thanked her for being such a great mom. She responded by breaking down and crying, and they had a long conversation. Ever since, Allen noticed an even greater improvement in their relationship as well as his ability to handle the grief and hardships of the divorce.

Allen said that he had to call me and tell me what happened. He was excited to see the real and dramatic impact of grace. Over a year later, Allen messaged me out of the blue to thank me. He wrote, "I talk of you often and the influence you have had, and your story."

I recently checked in with Allen as I neared the completion of this book, seven years after our first conversation. He is remarried and living fifteen minutes away from his ex-wife and her partner. While their story doesn't have a fairy tale ending, it's yet another story of the power and beauty of God's grace in a broken world.

Uncontainable Grace and Faith

Over the past ten years I have been caught in a wonderful spiral of grace. The more I practice extending radical grace, the more I want to express it and share the Good News, and then the more I practice extending grace. On and on it goes.

I have become uncontainable with my grace and faith, like Peter and John when they told the Jewish rulers who had just threatened and jailed them, "We cannot stop telling about everything we have seen and heard."[59] I have shared my grace story in countless conversations with people in grocery stores, hospitals, and on

[59] Acts 4:20.

college campuses. When I give my testimony to groups, it's not uncommon for someone to come up to me afterwards and tell me they just called a relative they had been avoiding for years or a former friend they'd become alienated from.

I've become unstoppable, and it's infectious to those around me. I seldom fret about not sharing my faith in Jesus; it simply happens because of the joy it brings to me and the hope it brings to others. It reminds of the something the prophet Jeremiah wrote:

> *But if I say I'll never mention the LORD or speak in his name, his word burns in my heart like a fire. It's like a fire in my bones! I am worn out trying to hold it in! I can't do it!*[60]

Imagine what kind of a place our world would be if more Christians had an uncontainable story. Ask God to help you experience and share yours.

---

[60] Jeremiah 20:9.

13 | Healing in the Bible

> And now, O Lord… give us, your servants, great boldness in preaching your word. Stretch out your hand with healing power; may miraculous signs and wonders be done through the name of your holy servant Jesus.
>
> Acts 4:29-30

In 1994, a sixteen-year-old boy named Billy Best sold some skateboard parts, baseball cards, and other belongings and fled his hometown of Norwell, Massachusetts, to avoid undergoing chemotherapy. He didn't tell anyone he was leaving or where he was going. The story became a national sensation.

Billy had been diagnosed with Hodgkin's Lymphoma and had undergone five chemotherapy treatments. He had lost twenty pounds and felt like the chemo was killing him. He had also seen his Aunt Judy suffer through chemotherapy and die. Billy was discovered in Houston, Texas, a month later and agreed to return home only after his parents promised not to make him go through any more chemotherapy. His doctors later sued his family to force him to undergo treatment, but a judge ruled in Billy's favor.

I read Billy's story in his book titled *The Billy Best Story* [61] in one day. I had never read a book in a single day before, but I was incredibly motivated. It was one of many cancer and healing-related books I either completely or partially read over the course of two years.

The thing that stood out to me was how Billy picked a treatment approach after deciding to forgo chemo. He had received so much media coverage that millions of people had heard about him, and a

---

[61] *The Billy Best Story, Beating Cancer with Alternative Medicine*, Billy Best & Linda Conti, Sandcastle Memoirs, 2012.

good number of them wrote letters to him. He had five shopping bags filled with them. It occurred to him that these were a great source of information, because many of them contained advice from people who claimed they had beaten cancer with "alternative" cures.

Billy initially thought many of these letters were from quacks, but the more he sifted through them, the more patterns began to emerge. He started to sort the letters into piles, and the pile that became the largest was from people who felt that diet had helped them beat their cancer. More specifically, he noticed that people urged him to eliminate four things from his diet: animal protein, dairy products, white flour, and sugar. Another thing that was mentioned repeatedly was the addition of Essiac tea.

To make a long story short, Billy heeded the advice in these letters, added one other thing to his self-prescribed treatment (a solution known as 714X), and has lived cancer free for over 20 years.

Billy had basically done a manual data analysis. While I'm unsure whether he precisely counted the number of letters that contained each of the treatments he chose to follow, it was clear to him that certain commonalities stood out when he sorted the letters into piles. His approach was simple yet powerful.

As I previously mentioned, I started gathering healing-related scriptures from the Bible not long after Diane was diagnosed. Reading Billy's story made me wonder if there was a way that I could analyze these passages for pearls of wisdom that could help Diane in her battle with cancer. Given the seriousness of her illness, I wanted to know if there was some way that Diane could experience a miraculous healing.

In particular, I wanted to answer the questions that were gnawing at me. For example, does God want Christians healthy like prosperity Gospel proponents claim? If so, why are so many them chronically sick? Does God make people sick and, if so, why? What were the purposes behind the miraculous healings so abundantly described in the New Testament?

As I collected scriptures in a Microsoft Excel spreadsheet, I assigned every passage[62] to one of four categories: those that describe a specific healing account, those that mention healing and/or health but don't describe a healing account, those that seem related to health and healing without specifically saying so, and those that are not healing related but are still worth considering. I looked at 330 passages of scripture in all.

Next, I started drilling down on the healing accounts to determine what each one said about who was healed, who did the healing, and what was the cause of the sickness. I paid attention to the outcomes and consequences of each account to get a sense for the purpose behind those healings.

For each healing account, I tried to note everything that was mentioned. For example, when Jesus healed a government official's son, I noted, among other things, that it was a specific healing account, that the healer was Jesus, that the sick person was healed because of the faith of a relative, that the healing was performed remotely, that the result was the healed person's family coming to faith in Christ, and that it was called a miraculous sign.[63]

After summarizing what the healing account data revealed, I turned my attention to healing-related scriptures to see what additional insight they added and then summarized my conclusions. Here is a very high-level summary of what I discovered:

High-Level Findings

Many biblically based arguments can be made that God wants to physically heal us. Here are four:

---

[62] From this point in, when I use the words passage, scriptures or verses it can mean anything from a single Bible verse to an entire chapter or two in the Bible.
[63] John 4:46-54.

- Jesus commanded His disciples to heal others and to teach future disciples to do the same, and every believer is a disciple of Jesus.
- Since God never changes, He is just as willing to heal people today as He was in early church times.
- Jesus brought the Kingdom of God to the earth, and there is no sickness in His Kingdom.
- God heals because that's who He is. He is "the Lord that heals."[64]

But the reality is that miraculous healing is exceedingly rare. There are several reasons for this, including weak faith, our fallen world and imperfect bodies, sin and the consequences of our sinful behavior, and the fact that Jesus only partially established God's Kingdom when He first came.

The last point merits extra focus. The Kingdom of God is somehow both present and future. While the powers of the Kingdom came into the world when Jesus first arrived, there is so much more to come when the Kingdom reaches its full consummation at his second coming. Yes, Jesus has taken our sicknesses and removed our diseases, but this will not be fully realized until His return. While He forgives all our sins and heals all our diseases as stated in Psalm 103, we continue to sin and get sick in this life and the full measure of our healing will not occur until His Kingdom is fully established.

The most-often mentioned effects and outcomes of New Testament healings are the following:

- They were miraculous, undeniable, awe-inspiring, and widely known.
- They aroused praise and worship of God.

---

[64] One of God's names is Yahweh Rapha, which means "The Lord that heals." See Exodus 15:26.

- They revealed who God is, i.e., a compassionate, merciful, and loving God.
- They demonstrated that love and compassion are more important than the law.
- They provided a foretaste of God's coming Kingdom, a Kingdom without sickness, pain, or death.

Also, Jesus and His disciples went out and engaged people, preached the Good News of God's Kingdom, and healed the sick. These things were tied together, both explicitly and implicitly. We have separated them to a large degree in Western Christianity, and we have become far more focused on our own miraculous healing than that of people who don't have a relationship with Christ. The focus on the healing of *others* to reinforce the message of the Gospel has been largely lost. It's no wonder such healing has become so scarce.

Prayer was part of only two of the fifty-one New Testament healing accounts. Jesus never prayed for anyone He healed, and He never asked God to heal them. He simply healed the sick. Only twice did one of His followers pray prior to healing someone. The contents of those prayers are unknown, and in both cases the healer performed another non-prayer action immediately preceding the healing.

On one occasion following a healing, Jesus indicated that certain types of healing require prayer and possibly fasting. He provided no instructions, though, for determining when this is the case or how exactly to pray.

The most common actions that were part of New Testament healing accounts were short, bold healing proclamations and commands, and some form of touch.

The faith of the sick person, a loved one, and the healer are all cited as factors in healings but each only a small number of times. If we consider acts of faith, like people coming to a healer and pleading to be healed, then faith is far more prevalent in New Testament healings. Finally, faith could be considered a prerequisite for healing if we make the reasonable assumption that all the New Testament healers (i.e., Jesus, His disciples, and a few other men of note) had great faith.

Repentance or the confession of sins are never mentioned as a factor in, or prerequisite for, New Testament healings, and only one New Testament healing account ends with the healed person being told to stop sinning. The apostle Peter did, though, tell a crowd to repent and believe following his healing of a Temple beggar.

A variety of ailments were healed in New and Old Testament healing accounts, and their seriousness is remarkable, including blindness, paralysis, and leprosy. In New Testament accounts, Jesus and his followers were not in the business of healing unseen, minor ailments while leaving those with obvious and profound conditions unattended. Quite the contrary, The New Testament emphasizes their focus on the most challenging health issues, including sometimes raising the dead, and healings were complete and swift.

Finally, there are both Old and New Testament examples of God making people sick, both directly and indirectly through some intermediary agent. Old Testament healing accounts provide much more detail on the causes of sickness than New Testament healing accounts. Most sicknesses described in these accounts were due to either sin and rebellion, punishment of Israel's enemies/oppressors, or God's desire to teach or affect something.

In summary, we need to move about in our communities, workplaces, schools, and world, sharing the incredibly Good News of God's coming Kingdom and Jesus' redemptive work, and boldly proclaim healing over those who are sick. This is the predominant context of healing throughout the New Testament.

When it comes to the healing of Christians, we should follow the admonition in the book of James to confess our sins to one another and to call on faithful elders to pray over us when we are seriously sick.[65] And we should never stop doing these things no matter who is healed or not. We should also ask God to activate the gift of healing[66] in us if we feel moved to do so.

The Bible's picture of good health accounts for our whole person, including our body, soul, and spirit. Only when you feed, exercise, detoxify, and otherwise care for each of these will you experience holistic good health. The Bible reveals a host of promises and linkages between things like prayer, examining the Bible, thanksgiving, and praise, and benefits like good health, peace, joy, and strength.

Observations and Conclusions

I have never seen someone miraculously healed of a serious condition like complete blindness, paralysis, or advanced terminal illness, and I have never seen anyone raised from the dead. I have also never been told by someone I deeply trust that they have either experienced such a healing or know someone who did.

I have attended a few healing conferences and seminars hosted by representatives from well-known healing ministries. I did not see anyone with serious illnesses like cancer or Alzheimer's healed at these events. There were, admittedly, people at these gatherings who claimed healing from various ailments, such as back pain or numbness in their legs. But nothing happened that mirrored the power, completeness, and speed of the healing that Jesus and His disciples were a part of.

Despite these experiences, though, I came away from my research and analysis believing more than ever in miraculous healing. The ongoing healing of my relationship with Diane led to a dramatic rise in my trust in God's Word. By following its mandate to love my enemy and to care unwaveringly for someone who had no interest in earning it, I saw how real and practical the Bible's

---

[65] James 5:13-18.

[66] 1 Corinthians 12:9,30-31.

teaching is about grace, and I committed to believe God's Word regarding everything, including healing.

As I studied healing in the Bible, I realized that the healing of our relationship with God dwarfs physical healing in importance. When we experience serious health problems, it affects us in a visceral way, and our physical suffering can easily become the dominant theme of our lives. But the Biblical truth is that no matter how sick we are in this life; nothing compares to what awaits us in God's Kingdom for *eternity* once our relationship with Him is restored. This knowledge should encourage us as we wrestle with illness in this lifetime.

I also realized that almost every healing described in the New Testament occurred in the context of the healers going out to people and sharing the Good News of God's coming Kingdom. Going, preaching, and healing were closely tied together—and they were commanded.

With respect to the healing of people who already believe in Jesus, there is not much insight to be gained from New Testament healing accounts. There are two New Testament accounts that explicitly mention a believer being raised from the dead. In one case, a kind, servant-minded woman named Tabitha was restored to life, and the news of her healing spread throughout her town and led many to believe in Jesus. In the second account, a young believer who fell to his death was raised up by the apostle Paul. The account says nothing more about the impact of that healing accept that people were greatly relieved.

Two sick believers are mentioned in the New Testament without any indication that they were healed. I'm not sure what to make of the discrepancy in outcomes between them and the two people who were raised from the dead.

As I stated earlier in this chapter, Christians have become overly occupied with their own health and wellness, and I see very few of them (including me) following the outwardly focused example of going, preaching, and healing that is so prevalent in New Testament healings.

Despite diving deeply into the topic of healing in the Bible for well over two years, I find that my thinking on the topic is still evolving to a degree. I have just recently begun to understand the importance of bundling preaching and healing together, and I'm just beginning to minister in this way to sick people I encounter as I move about in my community and workplaces. I'm also praying for wisdom regarding when to proclaim healing and when to pray for it, and I have done both for Diane.

Finally, I have asked God to activate the gift of healing within me, and I frequently offer up the prayer I shared at the beginning of this chapter while asking God to make miraculous healing more common in my community and around the world.

14 | Breaking Bad in Herndon

> This really sucks. Things are not OK. The worst part is the pain. I want to say this before it gets good for a while and then I don't say it. This phone call is to let you know I need help. I think God's lesson in this is accepting help. I had no clue how hard it would be to ask for and accept help. But let me see what I can do tomorrow before making any final decision about you moving in. (Laugh at the end.)
>
> Diane's comments to me during a
> late February 2018 phone call
> when she asked me to move in with her

Around Thanksgiving of 2017, as our daughter was preparing to return to school after spending a year at home, Diane received some bad news. Her CA-19 tumor marker had begun to rise. A tumor marker is a biomarker in your blood that correlates with an increase in tumor activity. This particular marker tracks well with pancreatic cancer tumor activity.

This put Diane in a bit of a foul mood during the holidays. Who could blame her? She had settled into a decent rhythm of life considering all she had been through, and I think we all let down our guards. Despite having endured twenty-eight chemo treatments that year alone, Diane was doing as well as could be expected, and she still looked great. Her healthy appearance was partly due to the beautiful, dense white hair that grew on her head following the Folfirinox treatments in 2016. Diane no longer cared about coloring her hair like she did prior to her illness. She was rockin' the gray!

While Diane's oncologist tried to ease her concerns that the rising tumor marker indicated a resurgence of her cancer, he agreed, at her insistence, to measure her CA-19 marker every two weeks. Over the next seven weeks, we watched Diane's marker rise six-fold to a level well out of the normal range.

We met with her oncologist again on January 4. Diane inquired about alternative treatments and the oncologist was clearly frustrated. In a detached manner he said things like, "You're likely progressing," and, "There's nothing else we can do." At one point, after she continued to press him, he said, "I don't make the rules," and, "You can go see another doctor."

I felt both sorry for him and pissed. I felt sorry because his standard of care had nothing to offer Diane beyond the loads of toxins they had already pumped into her chest port. He was at a loss. I was pissed for the very same reasons, and because his interaction with Diane was lacking in compassion. There was no hand holding or comforting or tenderness, even though we had clearly reached a major turning point.

Following the meeting, Diane and I went to her favorite coffee shop to chat about her options moving forward. I had felt compelled in the days prior to tell her how much I loved her and to thank her for being a great mom and wife.

At one point when she was talking, she choked up. Then I choked up. I reached out to grab her hand and thank her, and she said, "No, no, you'll make me cry." She looked away at first. I did it anyway and in a quivering voice and with tear-filled eyes, I told her I loved her and thanked her. Two young women at a table next to us were peeking at us periodically, trying to act normal. They probably hadn't imagined seeing such a deep exchange when they agreed to meet for coffee that day.

We also discussed how crappy the timing was in light of Shannon's plans to return to school just ten days later for her final semester of college. Within days of that coffee shop conversation, I would go for a walk and ask God to clearly show me if He wanted Shannon to return to New York. Despite me absolutely wanting her to stay home, it was obvious by the end of the walk that He wanted her back at school. Shannon and Diane agreed.

Back to Brooklyn

When the time came to drive Shannon to Brooklyn, we rented a minivan and loaded up all her belongings. I broached the topic of Diane staying home to rest while I took Shannon back several times, but Diane was having none of it. She was determined to take her baby back to school.

When the time came to head up the highway, and the van was completely packed, it was so crowded that Diane looked like an astronaut squeezed into a space capsule. She was jammed into a second-row seat and surrounded from floor to ceiling with Shannon's booty. She also had her personal baggage piled around her feet. This didn't faze her.

We arrived in Brooklyn around 6 p.m. and unloaded the car in frigid weather. Then we walked through the cold to one of Shannon's favorite Italian restaurants for dinner. We were all amazed at Diane's stamina. Regardless, I walked back to campus alone and drove the car to the restaurant to pick up Diane, Shannon, and Shannon's roommate. By the time Diane and I got to our hotel and went to bed, it was 2:00 a.m.

The next day was the day before my birthday, and the three of us went out to a favorite restaurant in SoHo to celebrate. Diane had grilled dorado fish, super smooth Italian wine, and we all shared baklava and profiteroles. The meal was amazing in every respect.

At one point, Diane talked about how her Italian aunt would get mad at her for sharing her cappuccino foam with Shannon when she was young, and here she was doing it again. I said, "We've been giving Shannon our foam in many ways for her entire life." We all had a good laugh. I felt so blessed to be able to share a meal like that, and I know Diane was happy to share it with Shannon before our return home. I was also glad to see Diane enjoy a meal. Eating had become an on-and-off struggle for her.

We drove Shannon back to school to drop her off. We knew we wouldn't see her before driving back to Virginia the following morning. I didn't even get out of the van when we got back to the campus because I knew I would be a crying mess if I hugged them both and said goodbye. Diane and Shannon said their goodbyes with much greater restraint, and Diane and I drove home the following morning.

I am convinced that Shannon's return to Virginia at the start of 2017 contributed mightily to the good year that Diane had, and I had to wonder if her return to school may have contributed in any way to the cancer progression Diane was now experiencing.

Last-ditch effort

Not long after our return home, Diane had yet another CT scan. This one confirmed our suspicion that her cancer had begun progressing again and was visible throughout her omentum. This, coupled with the absence of conventional treatment options, led us to dust off the alternative medicine research we had done. The good news was that Diane was now far more willing to consider such treatments. The bad news was that her immune system had suffered a great deal of abuse from thirty-nine chemo treatments spread out over a year-and-a-half, and her cancer was now quite advanced.

Diane had also begun to experience bouts of serious pain. They were intense but short-lived episodes that typically flared up after she ate. At first, they would slow her down and bend her over a bit, and later became so intense that they would stop her in her tracks. This was remarkable for a woman who had spent fourteen hours in labor when our daughter was born without making a peep, despite receiving a Pitocin drip and zero pain killers. This is when I began to realize how challenging her final months could be.

When Diane's tumor marker began to rise, I resurrected a spreadsheet I had developed that listed various treatment options. Nothing was beyond consideration. Now that it was clear that western medicine had nothing more to offer, I started updating the table in an attempt clarify Diane's choices.

Given how quickly Diane's cancer seemed to be progressing, I color-coded each treatment option according to its ease of implementation. Green indicated something with little-to-no barrier to implementation. Yellow presented barriers that would be easy to address. Orange included things that were doable but presented significant barriers. Red included treatments that were simply unavailable for one reason or another. We needed to move fast, and I wanted to rule out things that would be too difficult to implement.

There were several approaches I thought Diane should pursue, and I had been pushing for them for the better part of two years. These included a radical change in her diet plus fasting. Diane wanted no part of these things.

The cannabis documentary she had seen early in her cancer journey touted the efficacy of cannabis as a curative measure. She had been taking CBD oil since November 2016 and was now ready to do a full-on cannabis treatment that would include THC, the psychoactive and illegal component of cannabis. Cannabis treatment was code Orange in my table because of the significant legal and access barriers it presented. Diane didn't care. She was all in.

The gentleman we had retained to devise Diane's supplement regimen also happened to have significant expertise in the use of cannabis in the treatment of cancer. We had chatted with him just before we took Shannon back to Brooklyn, and there was a noticeable sense of hope and positivity during the call. He was initially surprised to even hear from us, and even more surprised to see how good Diane looked. He thought Diane had passed away. He said, "Patients like you doing well are rare in progressed pancreatic cancer. Don't wait until next month with a rising marker. Get moving. The oncologist has nowhere to go." He also quipped that his prescription pad said, "Maui."

Since cannabis had not yet been approved for medicinal purposes in the state of Virginia, Diane and I agreed that we would investigate the barriers to treatment in surrounding states. We also began contacting family, friends, and acquaintances about quickly moving to a location where Diane could legally access cannabis plant materials and high-potency oils. We were encouraged by Jared Smith's story.

A life-saving enterprise

At age twenty-seven, Jared Smith was diagnosed with stage IV glioblastoma, a form of brain cancer that is ranked as the deadliest of all cancers. Survival averages twelve to fifteen months following diagnosis, and only three to five percent of people with the disease survive five years.

During 2015, Jared received both radiation and chemotherapy treatments. He also improved his diet and even tried juicing for a while. But his tumor kept coming back.

In September of that year, the doctors told Jared and his family that all they had to offer was more radiation and chemo. They said Jared was likely in the end stage of his disease.

Jared's mom, Sally, was undeterred. She recalled hearing about the use of cannabis for disease treatment a few years earlier and began investigating. She soon came across an organization called New England Grass Roots Institute (NEGRI), a medical cannabis and holistic healing center outside of Boston.

Sally contacted Mike Fitzgerald, NEGRI's co-founder, and he sprang into action. NEGRI developed a high-potency form of cannabis oil that Jared ingested three times a day for six weeks. The result was remarkable. An MRI showed that Jared's primary tumor shrank over 50 percent while he was on the cannabis regimen. They continued the high potency treatment for another six weeks and the tumor continued to shrink. Then Jared switched to a lower "maintenance" dose.

Today, three years later, Jared is alive and well. He still has a tumor, but it is substantially smaller than its peak size and in a steady-state condition. He has adjusted his diet to strengthen his immune system, and he lives with his parents, two dogs, and a varying number of his sisters, depending on their travels.

Diane crossed paths with one of Jared's sisters at a Northern Virginia gym, and she strongly urged Diane to reach out to her parents to learn more about Jared's treatment.

On January 23, the week following our trip to Brooklyn, Diane and I were on a plane bound for Boston en route to the family's home in Massachusetts. When we arrived at the Smith house, we were greeted warmly by everyone, including a huge dog who literally tries to climb up people and hug them with his front legs.

We wound up spending over five hours with them that day. They were excited to share their experience and knowledge about cannabis. We spent most of the time walking through the process they use to reduce cannabis plant material to high-potency oil. This is necessary because of the high dosing needed in the use of cannabis as a curative measure.

We started by heating high-THC-content marijuana in an oven for forty minutes. This process is known as decarboxylation and is needed to activate the THC. This is why people light up a joint or a bong with a match to get high. Without heat, the psychoactive effects of the plant will not be released.

Next, Sally removed the stems from the plant matter and crumbled up the weed into a mason jar. She then added a copious amount of Everclear grain alcohol, sealed the jar, and shook it vigorously for five minutes. This step transfers about 80 percent of the THC from the plant material to the alcohol.

She then strained the contents of the jar through an Augbunny muslin bag into a 10" glass pie plate. This removed the plant matter so that all that's left in the pie plate is THC-infused alcohol. The pie plate was then set inside a similarly sized induction pan containing enough water to touch the bottom of the plate. Finally, the pan/plate combo was placed on a Nuwave induction cooktop set at 170 degrees.

For the next two hours we monitored and manipulated the alcohol as it slowly burned off leaving an increasingly small amount of thick oil behind. In the end, we had extracted five grams of high-potency oil from 1.3 ounces of cannabis.

Sally took two razor blades and carefully scraped as much of the oil as possible out of the pie plate into a small silicone container. The oil is incredibly sticky and difficult to deal with, which is why silicone is used to store it.

As we walked through the process, the family shared their journey with us and showed us their cannabis production facility. It was an impressive enterprise. In their basement they have two large enclosures where they grow the plants: one for seedlings and the other for larger, more mature plants. They also have a dry room upstairs. The dad, Gerry, even installed a system that cycles unused electricity back into their house to lower the cost of running humidifiers in the plant enclosures.

All of this was possible, of course, because growing cannabis for medicinal purposes is legal in the state of Massachusetts, and Gerry happens to run a construction business, so he's pretty good at these sorts of things.

In Virginia, cannabis was not legal at that time for *any* use. This was on my mind throughout our conversation. I kept thinking, *Where is this headed and what am I willing to do to help Diane with her chosen treatment approach*?

It was dark, rainy, and cold when we left the Smith house and headed back to Boston. At one point, I exited the dimly lit road we were traveling to get gas for our rental car. As I pulled up to the pump, Diane said, "I don't know what I would do without your help with all of this." Comments like that made everything worth it.

One gram or bust

The Smiths suggested that Diane begin dosing with an amount of cannabis oil equivalent to a half-grain of rice, and then ramp up over four-to-six weeks until she reached one gram. I would later discover that high dosing approaches like this have been described in medical literature.[67]

I watched several videos on cannabis oil and many of them stressed how potent even a tiny dose is. I figured a full gram, which filled most of a pill capsule, would be ridiculous.

Diane started dosing with cannabis on February 9, 2018. According to my calculations, her initial oil supply would run out in about three weeks. That meant she needed to quickly identify a source for significant amounts of cannabis. There were several obstacles in our way, the biggest including the illegality of cannabis in Virginia and the resultant lack of places where she could buy it.

The situation touched off a lot of angst in me. I spoke to lots of people and most of them didn't see an issue. One person literally said, "F*** the law! Diane is fighting for her life, so get the weed however you can." There were a smaller number of people who stressed moving forward with caution.

I happened to hear a sermon right around that time that was based on a scripture in Proverbs that says, "Wise people see trouble coming and get out of its way, but fools go straight to the trouble and suffer for it."[68] I thought of how I was almost always with Diane, taking her wherever she needed to go. I started envisioning my car getting impounded as I crossed state lines with bags of weed in the trunk, or me getting handcuffed after getting caught "cooking" in her apartment.

I sought the counsel of three separate pastors, and they all said the same thing, i.e., that love is more important than the law. They

[67] "Practical Considerations in Medical Cannabis Administration and Dosing," Caroline MacCallum and Ethan Russo, *European Journal of Internal Medicine*, 2018.
[68] Proverbs 27:12 (ERV).

pointed out the fact that Jesus healed on the Sabbath, a violation of Mosaic law.

We didn't have much time, so I established a couple of simple ground rules with Diane. I told her I would continue to drive her everywhere, but always in her car. I also told her I would never cook. In the end, supply was never an issue because Diane found a seller in Maryland who was also battling cancer with cannabis. And she didn't care one iota about the law. She was fighting for her life.

A Difficult Request

Some interesting things started happening as Diane ramped up her cannabis intake. One is that it became somewhat of a truth serum. One example is something she confessed to me one night while we were eating dinner together. She said she was awakened by a mistaken Skype call at 3:00 a.m. the night before. She confessed that, for some unexplained reason, she propped herself up on her elbow in bed after the call, looked around her room, and said, "God, this place is a mess." I was astounded when she admitted this to me. Her inclination to hold onto everything she ever acquired, and the resulting clutter, were a huge source of frustration for me in our marriage. She had never spoken so frankly before.

A more serious admission came on a Sunday night in late February. Diane called me and I captured her words in a notebook as she spoke. Those comments appear at the beginning of this chapter.

Diane intentionally called me while she was in pain to force herself to ask me to move in with her. I was surprised this was an issue, given that she had recently lived with me for three months following her apartment flood. But that was a situation where she literally had no other choice.

I told her not to let my occasional ungraceful behavior, or her not wanting to burden me, or her wanting to first organize her apartment get in the way of asking me to move in. I spent four of the next six days with her, and then moved into her apartment to live full time the following Monday.

Cooking

As soon as I moved in with Diane, she needed to prepare more cannabis oil. On the first day, we drove to Bethesda, Maryland, about thirty minutes from Diane's home, to meet a friend of hers and his wife for lunch. As we walked from the garage to the restaurant, Diane had a wave of pain that stopped her dead in her tracks on a busy sidewalk and had her wondering aloud if she could hold her bowels. I felt utterly helpless.

After the pain finally subsided, we met the couple and had a lovely lunch. It was a short-lived window of peace, though, as Diane was hit with another wave of pain as we walked back to our car. She kept plowing forward, though, and we drove to her supplier's home to pick up a couple of ounces of cannabis.

The next day was typical, with Diane sleeping late under the influence, and the day passing by faster than we wanted when she was up. The two of us started prepping the cannabis she had picked up the day before at about 6:29 p.m. It soon became evident that we had started too late for Diane. Just as we arrived at the point where the cannabis-laced alcohol was reduced to oil, Diane started conking out. Before I knew it, I was standing alone in the kitchen pushing the alcohol/oil combination around a pie plate with a silicone spatula. I was cooking despite saying I wouldn't, and there was little I could do about it.

There were moments when I got a little freaked out, like when some of the oil got stuck to my uncovered fingers, and when I thought I cut my finger with the razor I used to scrape oil from the plate. In the end, thank God, I managed to survive without getting stoned in the process.

Over the following few weeks, Diane's pain, weakness, and loss of appetite all intensified in parallel with her increased cannabis dosing. One night, Diane was sitting on the couch with her legs crossed yoga-like while a tear streamed down each of her cheeks. She said she didn't want to eat because of the pain. I thought, *God, this is awful.* On another day, Diane said the cannabis made her not want to move anything. Not her arms, legs, lips...anything. I couldn't imagine what she was going through.

Things weren't all bad, though. We had also begun to pray together nightly, and the prayers were beautiful and deep with lots of thanksgiving, despite the circumstances. Diane was a private person when it came to things like praying, so her invitation to pray together was heartwarming and affirming.

There were also amazing, funny moments, like her determination to get out of bed one morning at 8:00 a.m. to make a haircut appointment. I don't think Willie Nelson could have gotten up with the amount of cannabis oil in his system that she had, but she had her priorities.

We were fast approaching the six-week point that Diane had targeted to get a scan to confirm whether the cannabis treatment was working. Jared Smith had shown dramatic improvement in that timeframe, and we were hopeful that Diane's scan would show the same.

15 | Culminating Grace

Thank you, thank you, thank you.

Diane's words to me one night
as I tucked her in bed

In mid-March 2018, Diane and I visited the palliative care doctor in her oncologist's practice. She had ingested one gram of cannabis oil the night before and was walloped. While she hadn't experienced any hallucinogenic effects from the cannabis, it knocked her out every night. She was particularly groggy this morning because she had to get up at 7:30 a.m. to make the appointment on time. She had slept far less than the typical twelve or fourteen hours she had become accustomed to sleeping during her cannabis treatment.

The absence of psychoactive effects was evidently because she had been taking CBD oil for an extended period prior to introducing THC. I would monitor her state by occasionally asking if she had seen any aliens. Her answer was always the same. "No aliens."

Diane's stomach had been growing and was quite large and firm at the time of the appointment. She was uncomfortable. The doctor informed us that this was a condition known as ascites, and that her stomach would eventually and periodically need to be drained for relief—a procedure known as a paracentesis. I later looked up the condition on the Web, and an article I found said that ascites only affects 20 percent of pancreatic cancer patients, basically those people who had outlived the average lifespan of people with the disease. That was the good news. The bad news was that the article said that the onset of ascites usually heralds "imminent demise."[69]

---

[69] Emmanuel E. Zervos et. al., *Prognostic Significance of New Onset Ascites in Patients with Pancaracenreatic Cancer*, World Journal of Surgical Oncology, February, 2010.

I immediately thought, *What the heck do they mean by imminent?!* As I read further, the article said that patients who had undergone surgery lived no more than four weeks after the onset of ascites. Patients who had not had surgery survived "slightly longer."[70] Diane had not had surgery.

As we were preparing to leave the examining room on that sluggish Tuesday, I pointed out a hole in Diane's pants and teasingly asked if the jeans came with it. In a very loopy drawl she said, "I paid for that hole." Even amid her dazed, exhausted, and uncomfortable state, she still had a sense of humor.

The Search for Comfort

Ten days later, Diane had another CT scan. She requested this one to get a sense for whether the cannabis treatment was effective. It wasn't. Frankly, we didn't need a scan to tell us that, given the progression of her ascites and other symptoms.

Diane's scan results led to a lot of questions and self-doubt. Was the quality of the cannabis she used sufficient? Should she have spread her daily dosing over the course of each day? Did she ramp up to one gram too slowly? Does cannabis even work as a treatment for pancreatic cancer? These and many other questions swirled in my mind. We'll probably never know the answers.

Diane had her first paracentesis just two days before the scan. The procedure drained three liters of fluid from her stomach. Her relief was only temporary, though, and she felt the same amount of discomfort the day after the procedure that she had felt just before it.

Diane had challenges on several other fronts as well. Her pain had gone from short bursts one to three times per day to persistent pain that would last for hours. She had progressed from using Tylenol to Prednisone and was considering taking opioids. She had

---

[70] Ibid.

also stopped her high-dosage cannabis treatments and was now using it at lower dosages for symptom relief only.

One morning I went in to check on her at about 7:00 a.m. and found her awake and exhausted after being up and down all night with pain. She was on the verge of taking Oxycodone (Oxy). This was a big deal for her because she was seriously worried about its side effects. She asked me to pray with her and rested her head on my shoulder. I wept and prayed, snot dripping from my nose.

I felt overwhelmed and alone helping Diane. There was no one living with us to help me when issues arose in the middle of the night. I was really tired and sad to see Diane suffer. She said she couldn't even find a comfortable pain-free position that would allow her to sleep.

Diane started an Oxy regimen that morning and struggled to zero-in on a dosage that gave her relief. She said that her pain and other side effects were pervasive and permanent. She felt like she could never get away from them and that they had taken over every aspect of her life.

We would soon discover that the process of determining the proper Oxy dosage is more art than science. Too much Oxy and a patient can overdose. Too little and severe pain persists. Even worse, as the disease progresses, the amount, type, and location of pain all vary, which makes proper dosing even more difficult.

By the end of March, Diane was in a purely palliative mode of care. We were focused only on managing her symptoms and giving her the best quality of life during whatever time she had remaining. The following journal entry captures some of the challenges we were facing:

> *I went into Diane's room at 5:00 a.m. and she had been up with pain all night. She was miserable. She finally got comfortable at 6:00 a.m. and slept for four hours. We had an appointment today to get her second paracentesis, and the hospital called and canceled it via voice mail.*

Unbelievable. A combination of problems with the doctor's order, incorrect lab work, and questions surrounding her insurance coverage led them to remove it from the schedule. We decided to go to the emergency room at 3:00 p.m. After an hour-long wait, they told us they couldn't perform the procedure either. Diane sat and cried on the hospital gurney. We checked out. I got her cozy in the car and swung by the pharmacy to drop off a script. I took her home and she lay down. I went back out for the script and had to jack up $165 because of preauthorization issues. It just seems like there's one thing after another with our broken healthcare system. When I returned to Diane's apartment, I peeked in on her in bed and asked how she was feeling. She gently said, "Happy." It was worth a trillion dollars. It was one of those brief moments where she was free from pain, and I'm sure we both hoped it would continue forever. God bless her sweet soul.

Two days later, we visited Diane's oncologist. He strongly urged us to bring Shannon home from college as soon as possible—at least for a week. His mom had died from pancreatic cancer when he was twenty-three—Shannon's age at the time. He also urged Diane to sign up for hospice care and to get a permanent drain placed in her stomach.

After the appointment, I ran a few errands while Diane waited in the car, and then we drove back to her apartment along a scenic road we had been down many times before. As she marveled at the forsythia bushes and other blooming greenery, she said she had had a good life. When we got home, we had dinner while watching two episodes of a TV comedy series on the computer. Afterwards, we watched a movie together. It was the longest period I had seen her mostly pain-free in a while. The evening was as good as the previous evening had been bad. She would go on to have a rough night, though. She would later say, "I can't stand the nights."

<u>Home, Back, and Home Again</u>

Shannon returned to Virginia just two days after our meeting with Diane's oncologist. We were both so glad she was home. Her presence brought joy to Diane, and she took a great deal of pressure off me.

I also sent out a plea for help to the group of people I had been updating on Diane's condition via e-mail, and several folks began coming to visit with Diane, enabling Shannon and me to run errands and even take occasional breaks. This was not a panacea, though. There were times when I would leave instructions for giving Diane her painkillers while I was out, only to return and find that someone had neglected to give her the medicine at the proper time.

The three of us tried to do things that brought Diane joy whenever we could. A few days after Shannon's return, we drove to a gourmet pizza truck that Diane loved. The truck consisted of a pickup pulling a trailer containing a wood burning oven and food prep area. The owner, Harry, is a wonderful guy whom Diane had become close to over the past year. Harry worked with his dad, a gentle soul, whipping up handmade pizzas for the lunchtime and dinner crowds throughout D.C.

It was a gorgeous spring day with blue skies and puffy clouds and just a touch of coolness in the air. Diane, Shannon, and I sat on the tailgate of Harry's pickup while chatting with him through the trailer door as he and his father cranked out pizzas. Shannon and I enjoyed most of our pizzas, but Diane was unable to eat much. She was still very happy. We all had a wonderful time and I snapped numerous pictures of Harry, Diane, and Shannon.

The next morning as I lay in bed awake at 5:30 a.m., I realized no one had taken a picture of Diane, Shannon, and me. The more I thought about it the more heartbroken I became. I thought, *Why didn't I or anyone else think to do that?* I couldn't recall a recent, good picture of the three of us together, and I felt like we let a great opportunity to get one pass by.

I went to check on Diane and she was struggling with pain as usual. She also couldn't get her cell phone flashlight to work, which was frustrating her greatly. I wanted to talk about what was upsetting me, but she was suffering and upset herself. I got a heating pad cranked up for her and we sat and talked on her bed. She cried and said, "There's simply no peace." The importance of the picture seemed to fade.

Two nights later, Diane and I went to the emergency room at the suggestion of a hospice nurse whose services we had just retained. Diane had not had a bowel movement in eight days despite trying both an enema and a suppository, and both Diane and the nurse were concerned.

After we checked in, we were put in a large, fluorescent-lit room and waited as various doctors and nurses popped in and out. They eventually asked Diane to drink a large cup of oral contrast in preparation for a CT scan. This would be no small feat given her lack of appetite and nausea. I helped her to slowly drink the liquid over a forty-minute period, and she had a CT scan about two hours later. At around 3:00 a.m., they rolled Diane to another room and I could see the doctor reading her scan report on a nearby computer. He was engrossed and began making phone calls. At one point I heard him say the word "collapsed," and I got concerned. He soon noticed me watching him and moved to a computer further away.

When the doctor finally came into our room, he had some bad news. The scan revealed that part of Diane's colon had collapsed, and there were other "compressions" in her small intestine. The doctor said that there was nothing they could do about it. He said a complete collapse would warrant them draining her stomach, and then Diane would have to decide whether to get a colostomy bag or not. But since there was still a small amount of contrast getting through her colon, they didn't want to do anything right then.

I thought, *What an awful piece of news to receive!* Among all her other problems, she was now facing the prospect of never pooping normally again.

Diane and I got home around 4:00 a.m. Shannon was scheduled to go back to Brooklyn that day and, following some prayer and discussion, we all agreed that she would go back, try to wrap up her schoolwork as soon as possible, and return home again. She left for school later that day.

Within a few days, Diane threw up whenever she ate the smallest amount of food. I wrote the following e-mail update to our friends:

> *Diane's condition continues to worsen. Frankly, her drive to push forward given her lack of nutrition and sleep, the load of opioids she's taking, the faltering of her digestive system, and her increasing vomiting is astounding. It has become clear that she wants Shannon to get back home. This is all terribly draining, though, for her and me. This past week was especially bad. We were basically up all Saturday night a week ago at the ER, and we found it necessary to get up every three hours in the night since to take pain medication. It's a long story why, so I'll spare you the details. We plan to place a Fentanyl patch on Diane in about a half hour and are hoping this will allow her to sleep through the night and avoid forcing Oxy pills down her throat. Shannon is working hard to wrap up all her schoolwork and get back home to her mom. There appears to be little likelihood that Diane will be able to attend her graduation in mid-May, and there's a chance that Shannon and I won't be there as well. I've reached the point where I don't even care.*

Four days later, Shannon returned to Virginia. At about 2:30 a.m. that same morning, I checked on Diane and she was awake. She was a bit loopy and confused about Shannon's whereabouts. At first, she thought Shannon was back home but not in the apartment. Then she thought Shannon was en route on the train. I told her that

Shannon would be back later that day, and she asked me to reassure Shannon that she was at peace if she did not make it until then.

While Diane rallied for a few days with Shannon's return, her rapid decline was undeniable. On one night, she got sick four times between 3:00 and 11:00 a.m., and each time she was unable to make it to the bathroom due to her weakness. We made do using small trash cans and liners. Nights like that were both surreal and exhausting. Diane kept chuckling that Shannon always seemed to be alone with her when she was in good shape and joking around, and I was always with her when she needed help through a rough patch.

One night, as I was tucking Diane in bed and making sure she had everything she needed around her, she slowly raised her arms and put them around me while quietly and just as slowly saying, "Thank you, thank you, thank you." This made all the rough patches worth it.

Peace at last

On Thursday, April 26, Diane became minimally responsive in the late afternoon. While she couldn't move or communicate normally, she occasionally let out a grunt or moved her eyes or lips slightly. We appeared to be nearing the end.

Her sorority sisters had just visited the day before. Their timing was amazing. We spent a couple of hours sitting around Diane's dining table telling stories and laughing. When Diane became too weak to continue, I helped her slowly walk to her bed and get in. Diane sat upright in bed with her legs crossed while her friends surrounded her. One by one they spoke, prayed and cried. When they were all finished Diane said, "Why's everybody so sad. I'm okay!" She was smiling and upbeat.

On Thursday night, the hospice provider sent over a nurse to spend the night. She arrived around the same time that a wonderful acupuncturist finished treating Diane. The acupuncturist told me that, during a brief period of alertness, Diane had said that she was ready to die but her body wouldn't let her.

This made perfect sense to me given how hard Diane had pushed through everything for nearly two years. Earlier in the week I had gone into her room late at night and found her sitting upright. I gently told her to lean back and get some rest, but she didn't budge. She was supported by her left arm extending back to the bed and I gently tried to move it and lean her back. She still wouldn't budge. I began exerting more and more force to move her arm, and finally gave up. I called Shannon in the room and she was able to coax her to lean back. I told Shannon that it was like trying to move a steel beam when I attempted to shift her arm. We fondly refer to Diane as "steel beam" every so often these days.

The next morning, Susan, Diane's little sister from her college sorority, came to spend the day. Susan is a hospice nurse by profession, and she was part of the core posse of sisters who had been so supportive through Diane's journey.

Susan spent the entire day at the apartment and was a huge help. Toward the end of her visit, she suggested that we clean Diane up before she left. It was at this point that we discovered a rather large bed sore on Diane's backside and lower back. I was distraught. I had seen what an advanced bedsore had done to my dad following hip surgery and extended stays in hospitals and rehab facilities. I reacted quite visibly, and I got the sense that this upset Diane. I couldn't believe no one had seen this yet, but Susan told me that these sores can appear quickly when someone is in a highly weakened end-state like Diane. She was trying to give me some peace.

A different nurse from the hospice service arrived to spend the night just before Susan left to go home, and it was immediately apparent that this nurse didn't want to exert herself. As Susan tried to share recommendations for treating Diane's bedsore with her, the nurse sat slouching in a chair, barely acknowledging her. It was so bad that I called the hospice service, which attempted to get her to be more engaged in Diane's care. I could tell that the nurse was annoyed with me for pushing her, and everything she did from that moment on she did lazily and with a scowl on her face.

This was crushing to me. I wanted Diane to get the best attention possible, and I was facing a long stretch of time with someone who didn't seem to give a crap. This kicked off a long, sleepless night during which I monitored the nurse as much as I monitored Diane.

At around 5:00 a.m., the nurse and I repositioned Diane to give her bed sore some relief. Each time she was shifted, Diane would struggle with fluids in her throat for five or ten minutes as she settled into a new position. She was unable to get these fluids out of her mouth in her minimally responsive condition, and it was tough to hear her suffer, even for a short period of time.

I was thrilled that the lazy nurse would soon be leaving and that a far more competent one was scheduled to arrive in the morning. It would be a couple of hours before the current nurse left, though, and I thought there was no sense trying to go back to my bed. I decided to squeeze in bed with Diane and the many pillows we were using to position her. We lay facing each other. I held her hand in mine and tried to get a little sleep. It was wonderful.

A new nurse showed up around 10:00 a.m. I got the immediate sense that she was very good at her job. She attempted to take Diane's vitals but found it difficult. She said she thought Diane only had a few hours to live. Despite Diane's condition, this was a bit of a surprise.

We cleaned and dressed Diane's sore together and got her repositioned. A short while later the nurse said, "She's going now, in the next few minutes." I was stunned. I thought, *How does she know this*?

Shannon got on the bed near Diane's arms and I got on next to her legs. The hospice nurse was behind her. We gently massaged Diane's arms and legs and told her we loved her and were proud of her and thanked her. And within a matter of minutes, just as the nurse had said, Diane was gone.

16 | Insights

- Ed's superior (holier than me) attitude has pushed me away from God. On the other hand, his horrible behavior has turned me to God since I feel so hopeless and have nowhere else to turn.
- Ed can be very arrogant. For all his Bible study, he is not very humble.
- Ed is like Dr. Jekyll and Mr. Hyde. I never know what kind of mood he will be in. Sometimes his bad moods last for days when he barely talks to me.
- Ed curses and carries on in his office making me feel sick and nervous.
- Ed has trouble controlling his anger.
- Ed criticizes me often. I do little that pleases him.

Diane's notes about me
three years before filing for divorce

I want to make one thing abundantly clear before sharing the insights I have gained from my journey. I am NOT the hero in this story. Jesus is.

Ed Melick is sinful, deceived, selfish, angry, and ugly. Jesus Christ in Ed Melick is perfect, truthful, graceful, peaceful, and beautiful. When someone sees me extending radical grace, that's not me. That's Jesus.

I can't tell you how many times someone has said to me, "I could never do that" after I told them my divorce story. My answer is always the same. "You're correct," I say, "You can't. But Jesus Christ can."

The observations at the beginning of this chapter are a small outtake from a list Diane wrote back in March 2005, three years before filing for divorce. They are true. Every one of them. I cringe when I see the date because it makes me realize how long I was misbehaving in my marriage. I also cringe at how lengthy the rest of the list is.

Now for the insights.

Sin and Deception

Many years ago, God spoke through the prophet Jeremiah saying, "The human heart is the most deceitful of all things, and desperately wicked. Who really knows how bad it is?"[71]

Human beings have an infinite capacity for self-deception. Just think of how you react when someone tells you something bad about yourself. Most people don't even bother sharing candid feedback with their friends and family because they know it might seriously damage or even end their relationship. We are skilled at seeing the faults of others but typically blind to our own. This is why Jesus spoke about dealing with the log in our own eye before trying to help our brother with the speck in his.[72]

I gained keen insight into the level of my own self-deception when Diane told me she was leaving me and that insight has been growing ever since. This is not the most pleasant process, but it's supremely worthwhile. Nowadays, when I screw up and misbehave, I'm much more willing to simply admit that such behavior reveals my sinful human nature. It's great to be free from the burden of trying to act like I'm better than I really am and of covering up my bad behavior with excuses. It's also joy-giving to point out the source of whatever goodness I display, which is Jesus Christ.

---

[71] Jeremiah 17:9.

[72] Luke 6:41-42.

We are all sinners and in the same boat. We like to believe that the sin of others is worse than our own, but the Bible teaches that if we have committed one sin, we have committed them all.[73]

If you really want to bring about major change in your relationships, you must start by recognizing, confessing, and repenting of your own sin. This leads you to be more humble, transparent, willing to forgive and accept others, and willing to accept critical feedback.

At the end of Diane's memorial service, I caught the speaker's attention and told him I wanted to say a few words. This was completely unplanned, and I had prepared nothing to say. I stood up and first thanked everyone for their help. I was so choked up I could barely speak, so I had to say *thank you* twice.

Then I pointed to a picture of Diane on the screen behind me and said, "This was grace, and I stomped all over it." I then began to talk about how our relationship turned around as I surrendered increasingly to the control of God's grace in my life.

I am still shocked at what I said, just like I was when I told Diane that I loved her and was proud of her ten years before in the bedroom of her new apartment. Moments like these are proof of Jesus' presence in me, and they are impossible without humility and repentance. This should be our starting point before doing anything else.

Change Yourself. Love Others.

For the last several years of my marriage, I was constantly blaming Diane for my frustrations with our relationship. This is incredibly common. I have spoken to countless unhappily married people and they spend their time talking about the faults of their spouse. They almost never acknowledge their own flaws.

---

[73] Romans 3:23, James 2:10, 1 Kings 8:46.

People like this also do all sorts of relationally unhealthy things like yelling, nagging, complaining, and criticizing to get their spouses to change. That never works.

I have often heard it said that you can't change other people, only yourself. I agree with this to a degree. But that's only part of the story. My experience showed that while I couldn't *make* Diane change, I could heavily *influence* her through my good and bad behavior.

Here's a simple example. One day, a few years into our divorce, Diane called and asked me to help her with her computer. That alone is shocking given my unhappy history with the machine and the terrible fight we had when she found me working on it just before the divorce and custody settlement.

I told her I would do my best to help but also said that I found it difficult to do given all the stuff that was piled around it. It makes it hard for me to think clearly. I said all of this in a decidedly different way than I used to, that is, calmly and lovingly.

Later that day, I stopped by to pick up Shannon and discovered that Diane had cleaned up the entire desk area surrounding the computer. It looked pristine. I wound up fixing the problem in about fifteen seconds because I could see things clearly and troubleshoot. We were both happy.

In the old days I would have ranted and raved about the papers, supplies and other "junk" around the computer, a fight would have ensued, and nothing would have gotten fixed. Now Diane was cleaning things up without me explicitly asking her to do so.

My decision to allow Christ to express His grace through me had a huge influence on Diane. It led her to begin trusting and listening to me again, with little things like the computer, and with big things like helping her devise a strategy when her job was in peril. I had earned the right to be heard again.

Thoughtfulness

When I look back on my marriage, I'm struck by how incredibly thoughtless I was regarding Diane and our relationship. I never paused to really think about why she struggled in certain areas, how her upbringing had affected her adult life, how to speak her "love language," or how to help her with her weaknesses and sensitivities. I also failed to consider my selfishness and its effect on her or the purpose of marriage beyond simply satisfying my own selfish needs and desires. And this thoughtlessness eventually led to heartlessness.

Here's one example. Diane's mom was a mean-spirited and manipulative woman who was very open about the fact that she regretted getting pregnant with, and giving birth to, Diane. Diane shared with me on numerous occasions that her mom had often told her that she was unwanted. To make matters worse, Diane's parents were both alcoholics who fought often, especially during dinner. This often gave Diane abdominal pain and made her sick.

When I began to grow in my displeasure with Diane and to treat her poorly, it had a greater impact on her than if she had grown up in a more loving home. I learned this from a counselor who was co-hosting a Hope for the Separated class I took not long after Diane left me. When she told me this, I was heartbroken that I had compounded the damage that Diane's mom had done. It also occurred to me that I had given no serious thought to these sorts of things.

Diane and I also failed jointly when we dove into our marriage without recognizing the need to feed and nurture our relationship. We were deep in the throes of romance and couldn't see any dangers ahead. When we got married, we viewed the pre-marriage counseling as a necessary nuisance. *We don't need counseling*, we thought. *We'll never have any issues*. As our years together grew, we never attended any kind of marriage booster event nor did we study how to keep our marriage healthy.

We were also woefully ignorant regarding the actual purpose of marriage. A friend recently said to me, "You don't get married because you fall in love. You get married to learn how to love."

I had never heard such a thing either in or out of church. What I did hear was that marriage is an earthly image of the union between Jesus Christ and His church.[74] But what that meant in practical terms escaped me.

It wasn't until I heard one particular sermon on marriage that things clicked for me. The pastor quoted God's commandment as written in Ephesians, "Husbands, love your wives, just as Christ loved the church."[75] And what did Christ do for the church, he asked? He laid down his life to the point of dying a horrible death, and He was radically forgiving as He did so.[76]

The pastor said that when men ask him if they need to do things their wives are pushing them to do, like come home from work at a reasonable time and help with the kids, the pastor always asks them if it's as bad as death. The obvious answer is no. Then he admonishes them to do the things that are important to their wives.

I learned to "die to self" and examine what was important to Diane and serve her. Here are some suggestions for how to be more thoughtful:

- Study what the Bible says about the meaning and purpose of marriage.
- Study how to feed and nurture your marriage and put into practice what you learn. Do things like going to your church's annual marriage booster and reading well-regarded books like *Love and Respect*, by Emerson Eggerichs. Make this an ongoing practice throughout the *entirety* of your marriage. Don't ever think you have

[74] Ephesians 5:21-33.
[75] Ephesians 5:25.
[76] Luke 23:34.

arrived and don't need to keep learning about your spouse. That's right when trouble begins.

- Spend time alone together. Schedule a weekly date night and take short trips if possible.
- Learn each other's "love language"[77] and "speak" them to each other.
- Give serious thought and prayer to the things about your partner that annoy you and ask God for wisdom and grace to react to annoyances in a Christlike manner.
- Do the things that are important to your spouse and do them willingly and happily.
- Reflect on moments when you screw up and ask for grace to grow from them and change. Realize how deeply your words damage, even on one single occasion.
- Develop a high-quality support community.

Community

One of the biggest lessons I learned from my divorce is the importance of community in our lives. Over the second half of my marriage, I became increasingly isolated. I simply had no close, quality friendships. This tendency toward being alone is more common that you might think, especially in this day of social media saturation.

When I think of the impact that my first men's retreat had on me and the friendships that it launched, I'm convinced that life would have played out differently in my marriage if I had been surrounded by faithful men who weren't afraid to call out and challenge my bad behavior. I even know some men who have what they call a marriage mentor, usually an older friend with a long, solid

---

[77] This term was popularized by Gary Chapman in his book *The Five Love Languages*.

marriage, whom they meet with periodically for advice. I have made the development of such friendships a priority.

I also had subtler revelations about community. For example, I prayed many times that God would release Diane from behaviors and character flaws that I thought were preventing her from healing and prospering. Some things I saw correctly; many I didn't.

Toward the end of her life, though, I began to realize that God seldom answered those prayers for change in her, me, and others. Instead, what I saw was an opportunity for flourishing through community. If Diane struggled with certain challenges, it was our responsibility to come alongside her and, in a sense, fill her voids with the abilities God gave us. Conversely, Diane could fill holes/weaknesses in our lives.

I stopped asking God to change people and began asking him to show me how I could fill the gaps in the lives of others and accept the help of others as they filled the gaps in my life. I committed to joyfully and thankfully do for others what they struggled to do for themselves, and gladly recognize and accept help from others in areas where I struggle. What a liberating thing this is, and a clever way that God drives us to community.

Hope and Commitment

I never lost hope that my relationship with Diane could be restored, and I committed to live according to that hope.

About three months after our divorce was finalized, I went to my third men's retreat. During one session, the speaker challenged the men to find out what their God-given name is, the name that indicates their higher purpose. As I stood up following his speech, I found myself face-to-face with an elderly gentleman whom I respect a great deal. He reached out and gently grabbed me by my upper arms. He looked deeply into my eyes and said that God had just told him that my name was "Diane's husband." His comment reduced me to tears. It was one of a long series of encouragements God gave me that propelled me to honor my marriage vows over ten years of legal separation. I never went on a single date in all that time nor did I become intimate with another woman.

As the years went by and our relationship was rebuilt, people started asking me if we planned to get remarried. While we didn't, mainly because Diane didn't seem to have any interest in doing so, people could see that something unusual was going on. Then an interesting thing happened near the end of Diane's life. We were visited in her apartment by three young adults who had offered to pray for Diane, and things got very deep. At one point, Diane looked at me and said, "I thought a number of times over the years that it would have been nice if we stayed together and helped each other out." This was a huge admission from Diane, who typically kept her feelings to herself. One of the young adults cried out, "We can marry you now!" We all laughed at the idea and then moved on to other topics, but I remained struck by Diane's comment.

In the end, I didn't need a marriage license from the county or the proclamation of a minister. We were husband and wife in spirit and action, and that's all that matters.

In the days following Diane's passing, a friend wrote to me saying, "There was no greater example of 'til death do us part' than your obvious love and devotion to Diane." It was clear to her that I was, indeed, Diane's husband.

Don't Expect a Hollywood Ending

Not long after my divorce was finalized, a friend gave me a copy of the movie *Fireproof.* The story is about a young couple headed for divorce. The husband decides to perform an act of love and kindness for his wife every day for forty days, regardless of how she responds. Toward the end, when she realizes he did something uncharacteristically selfless and sacrificial for her ailing mother, she rushes to see him, and they are reunited. The movie ends with them renewing their wedding vows in a park on a beautiful day.

I found myself occasionally envisioning a similar storybook ending to my divorce with Diane. But that didn't happen. Instead, our relationship ended with Diane drawing her last breath as I gently stroked her leg and told her that I loved her and was proud of her.

The ending was gritty, painful, and difficult, but beautifully so. While it wasn't what I would have chosen, it was a far more compelling demonstration of God's grace than I could have imagined, and a confirmation of His wisdom.

I Wasn't Perfect, and You Won't Be Either

Despite all the beautiful experiences described in this book, I was never perfect. Even on my best days, I had bad moments. Just two days before Diane passed away, I became verbally and visibly frustrated at the clutter in her bedroom as we tried to make space for a nurse to sit with her overnight. I'm not proud of that moment, and I wonder what Diane was thinking as she lay minimally responsive in her bed. I take comfort from the following scripture, though, when I slip up like this:

> *We now have this [glorious light of the Good News] shining in our hearts, but we ourselves are like fragile clay jars containing this great treasure. This makes it clear that our great power is from God, not from ourselves.*[78]

We are all fragile clay jars. We are imperfect humans. But don't let your mistakes discourage you from expressing the grace of Jesus Christ the way I strove to do over the past ten years. It is supremely worth it.

---

[78] 2 Corinthians 4:7.

17 | Healing Grace

> I thought this card was appropriate with the chemistry lessons we've had to learn because of my stupid cancer! Thank you for always loving me and for all you do for me! Love, Diane.

Valentine's Day card from Diane to me
picturing a chemistry set on the cover
Winter 2018

I hope it's become clear that God's grace is all about healing. First and foremost, it heals our relationship with God. By grace we are saved from a death penalty when we believe in the sacrifice of Jesus Christ for our sins and rebellion.[79] This is a sacrifice that Jesus made for every one of us. You and me.

This is truly divine healing with eternal consequences. Everything else pales in comparison. A person could live an absolutely miserable life on this earth, filled with illness and suffering, but that pales in comparison to the glorious future that lies in store for followers of Jesus Christ. The apostle Paul summed this up beautifully when he wrote:

> *For our present troubles are small and won't last very long. Yet they produce for us a glory that vastly outweighs them and will last forever!* [80]

Paul was no stranger to trouble. In the same letter he wrote about how he was imprisoned often; whipped and beaten countless times; stoned once; shipwrecked three times; adrift at sea for a day and a

[79] Ephesians 2:8 and John 3:16.
[80] 2 Corinthians 4:17.

night; confronted with danger from rivers, robbers, and enemies; often sleepless; sometimes hungry, thirsty, under-clothed, and shivering; and confronted with death on numerous occasions.[81] Yet he called these things small and temporary.

Paul knew that eternal life and an unimaginable future await those who believe the Gospel.[82] God is going to give us new, imperishable bodies—full of power.[83] There will be no more war, fear, illness, pain, sorrow or suffering. Peace, quietness, and confidence will fill the land.[84] God will literally give us everything.[85]

God's grace also heals our relationships when we extend love, service, forgiveness, kindness, and sacrifice to those who don't deserve it or cannot earn or pay for it. When Diane and I separated, we were enemies. Make no mistake about it, most people are enemies when they divorce. When God gave me a glimpse of His grace on that long weekend when I helped her move out of our home, He showed me the power involved in loving my enemy as we are commanded to do. This made me yearn to extend that grace to anyone and everyone.

After Shannon and I shut down Diane's apartment and moved into our current home, I stumbled across the Valentine's Day card Diane gave me a couple of months before her passing. The card had a picture of a chemistry set on the front along with the words *We've got amazing chemistry*. Inside she wrote, "I thought this card was appropriate with the chemistry lessons we've had to learn because of my stupid cancer! Thank you for always loving me and for all you do for me! Love, Diane." The last line is priceless and proves the reality, power, beauty, and impact of God's grace. Diane recognized that I chose to never stop loving her and to serve her

---

[81] 2 Corinthians 11:23-27.
[82] Romans 6:3.
[83] 1 Corinthians 15:42-43,48,52-53 and 2 Corinthians 5:1-10.
[84] Isaiah 2:2&4, 32:17, and 35:4-6&10; Hosea 2:18; Micah 4:4; and Revelation 21:3-4.
[85] Romans 8:32.

throughout our ten years of separation and divorce, especially during the most challenging period of her life.

Finally, grace heals physically. It's God's grace that heals people, good and bad, when they cut their fingers and the wounds clot and heal. It's God's grace that enables the immune system to constantly work to rid the body of toxins and infections. It's God's grace that gives doctors, scientists, and inventors the wisdom to invent treatments and technologies that heal the sick. It's God's grace that heals us physically when we forgive others, rest in the hope we have in God, and seek to know and obey God. It's God's grace that supernaturally heals some people against all odds when they are gravely ill. All these things and more represent God's miraculous grace in action.

Famous for Love

As I look back on everything that has happened, I think of two scriptures that I quote often. The first was part of a prayer that Jesus offered to his Father shortly before his crucifixion. He said, "May [my followers] experience such perfect unity that the world will know that you sent me and that you love them as much as you love me."[86] In the second, he told his disciples, "Your love for one another will prove to the world that you are my disciples."[87]

Our love for one another and unity among believers should make a powerful statement to the world. We should, as my pastor recently put it, be "famous for love." When I reviewed the many notes that people sent to me just before and after Diane passed away, the truth of this really struck me. People wrote that they have been blessed by my love and faithfulness to Diane, and that Diane touched many lives through me. One person wrote:

---

[86] John 17:23.
[87] John 13:35.

This was truly a story of God's grace, love and redemption and I'm thankful that you were open enough to share with us. Even if God didn't answer your prayers the way you hoped or move the mountains in your path, you held on strong to Him. Many folks would have turned their back, but you knew there was something bigger at play, and I hope your story inspires others to know that our God is a good God who provides us with not what we want but what we need.

I can hardly believe it's my journey people wrote about, especially considering how low I had sunk in my behavior while married. It reminds me of when Jesus said, "Now that you know these things, God will bless you for doing them."[88] He had just finished washing the feet of the disciples whom He knew would soon abandon him and probably the feet of the disciple who would betray him. I also chose to "do these things" when Diane left me and for ten years since, and I've been richly blessed.

I often challenge people to do the same. I ask them to identify the most difficult person in their life and to begin serving that person without wavering and watch what happens. Sadly, far too few people have accepted that challenge. This is unfortunate. We have infinite and unimaginable power at our disposal: the grace of God. We can put it to work *whenever we choose*. All we must do is make that choice and follow through.

The Fifth Thing

You may recall that I began asking God for five things in my marriage just before it was ripped apart eleven years ago. When I looked at the list about three years ago, I realized I had the first four of those things without even being married. That was pretty amazing.

[88] John 13:17.

Then I looked at the list again as I was writing this final chapter. The fifth item was as follows: *God, please bring us out of this period with a better marriage than ever, one with Jesus Christ at the core, deeply changed for the better and able to help many others.* I think He answered that prayer in a big way. My new prayer is that God would use our story to powerfully impact countless marriages and other relationships.

A Note about Christians

Despite being a "Christian" for over twenty years, I had allowed bad behavior to slowly and insidiously creep into my marriage until I reached a point where I was continually expressing displeasure with my wife. This is a terrible and shameful thing to realize and admit.

The Good News of the Gospel is that I'm forgiven these sins. My experience drove home the fact that Christians are, and always will be in this lifetime, sinners like everyone else. The ongoing battle with our sinful nature is a core aspect of the Gospel.[89] God calls sinners, not those who "think" they are righteous.[90] Christians *are* going to make mistakes, and sometimes they are big mistakes spread out over long periods of time. But this doesn't invalidate the truth and beauty of the Gospel. It actually supports it. It's part of a lifelong process that God has promised to complete in each of us.[91]

I can't tell you how many people I have hurt or misbehaved in front of in my life. I'm a mess. We're all messes, aren't we? But this is what makes grace so amazing. Despite being messes, we can do other-worldly things if we surrender to Christ's control in our lives. When I do mess up, I'm not as ashamed as I used to be. I embrace it because it reminds me that I'm a sinner and I don't need to act like I'm better than I really am. It also makes it obvious that

---

[89] See Galatians 5:17.
[90] See Matthew 9:13.
[91] See Philippians 1:6.

it's not me who is accomplishing great things when I extend radical grace, but rather Christ *in* me.

18 | The Gospel of Grace

> But my life is worth nothing to me unless I use it for finishing the work assigned me by the Lord Jesus—the work of telling others the Good News about the wonderful grace of God.
>
> Acts 20:24

I once heard a missionary speak at an event where he held up a bottle of water and exclaimed, "This is water. It's perfect. It's always refreshing and always good for you. It has no calories. It cleanses you internally, and when you bath in it you feel clean and refreshed." Then he held up a can of Coke and said, "This is also water, but we've added a bunch of stuff to it. The more of it you drink, the sicker you get. It'll make your teeth rot, eat a hole in your stomach, and make you fat. If you bath in it, you'll feel sticky and awful." He held up the water bottle again and said, "This is Jesus Christ." Then he held up the Coke can and said, "This is Christianity."[92]

I have never heard a better explanation of what ails Christianity. It seems that we've added so much garbage to Jesus that we barely recognize Him or understand His core message, the Gospel. What we have created is quite harmful. This fact coupled with what I've learned about true healing has led me to conclude that I simply can't write this book (or *any* book for that matter) and not include a description of grace and the Gospel.

---

[92] Jamie Winship speaking at Christian Fellowship Church in Ashburn, VA on March 25, 2011.

Love and justice

God is creating a family, and He is doing it through us.[93] At the outset of this process He placed the first two people He created (Adam and Eve) in paradise (the Garden of Eden). He gave them everything they could possibly desire and imposed only one single rule on them. The consequence of violating that rule would be deadly, and He clearly told them that.[94]

We similarly set limits on our kids all the time for their health, safety, and well-being. When they begin to crawl, we try to keep them from sticking their fingers in electrical sockets and swallowing house cleaning products to prevent them from being injured or killed. Do babies comprehend why we set limits on them and the dire consequences of violating them? Of course not. But that doesn't take away from their reality and importance, and the serious consequences of violating them.

It was much the same for Adam and Eve, and it's the same for us. We don't fully comprehend why sin is so terrible or its deadly consequences, but that doesn't make these things untrue or unfair. It demonstrates two key attributes of God: His perfect love and His perfect righteousness. God is so just that He simply cannot allow sin to go unpunished, yet He loves us so much that He provided a substitutionary sacrifice for each of us that is amazingly simple to claim.

When Adam and Eve disobeyed their one rule, sin and death entered humanity and our hearts became deceitful and rebellious.[95] This deceit and rebellion leads us to make poor choices that lead to sickness and unhappiness, and eventually death.[96]

---

[93] 1 John 3:1, Ephesians 1:5, Galatians 3:26 and 4:4-5, Romans 8:14,19,21,23; Matthew 5:44-45, Hebrews 14:15, Genesis 1:28 and 9:1, and Jeremiah 29:6.

[94] Genesis 2:15-17.

[95] Romans 5:12, Jeremiah 17:9, Romans 8:5.

[96] Romans 6:23, John 3:16, Matthew 10:28, 2 Peter 3:9, Galatians 6:8, John 10:28, Psalm 145:20, Psalm 1:6, Psalm 37:9,20, Deuteronomy 30:15-18, Revelation 21:8, 1 Corinthians 1:18, John 17:12, Psalm 73:27, Acts 20:26, 2 Corinthians 4:3, Genesis 2:16-17, Philippians

But God loves us so much that He was willing to provide a way out for us—one that doesn't depend on how good we are or how hard we work.[97] And the price He paid was higher than we could imagine. He sent His one and only Son to take on human form, live a life of hardship, and be horribly beaten, humiliated, and crucified.[98] He did this to pay sin's death penalty for anyone who accepts it. It's the ultimate expression of grace.

This is the essence of the Gospel. If we simply recognize, confess, and repent of our sinful natures, and accept the sacrifice of Jesus Christ to pay the penalty for our sins, we are forgiven every sin we have committed and will ever commit. Our death sentences are removed. We are adopted into God's family with all the rights and privileges that come with it, and we are given eternal life. This is truly divine healing, and everything else pales in comparison.

Grace defined

The word "grace" has been described as "the last best word" because it seems to be the only theological term that hasn't been spoiled.[99] Words like *gracious*, *grateful*, and *gratuity* hint at its meaning along with expressions like *saying grace*, *grace period*, and *grace notes*.

I've heard many definitions of grace. The simplest Biblical definition is the unmerited favor of God. This minimal definition, though, doesn't begin to capture the full meaning and impact of grace. Grace in its most powerful form is the supernatural thing by which a follower of Jesus Christ receives eternal salvation/life. This "saving grace" is mind-blowing stuff and is captured beautifully in the following Bible verse.

3:18-19, 2 Thessalonians 1:9, Ezekiel 18:4 and 20, 1 Timothy 6:16 (God alone can never die).

[97] Ephesians 2:8-9.

[98] Philippians 2:5-8.

[99] Philip Yancey, *What's So Amazing About Grace?* Grand Rapids, Michigan: Zondervan Publishing House, 1997, Page 12.

> *God saved you by His grace when you believed [in Jesus' sacrifice]. And you can't take credit for this; it is a gift from God. Salvation is not a reward for the good things we have done, so none of us can boast about it.*[100]

Saving grace has nothing to do with how good a person is and everything to do with the ultimate expression of God's perfect love for us.

Grace has other supernatural properties as well, like illogically working best through our weakness,[101] being the source of a Christian's strength,[102] and acting as the conduit through which God works through believers in Christ.[103]

There are also other more common forms of grace, as we touched on earlier. The Bible shows how God expresses grace when He gives sunlight and rain to both the evil and the good,[104] vision to both the poor and the oppressor,[105] and food for everyone to enjoy.[106] He is good to everyone, even kind to the unthankful and wicked.[107] People also express this grace when they extend love, service, forgiveness, kindness, and sacrifice to those who can't earn it or don't deserve it. We are capable of such grace because we are made in God's image.[108] These common forms of grace are often referred to unsurprisingly as "common grace."

Some people have gone as far as to describe grace as shocking and scandalous[109] given how incredibly counter it is to human nature and our notions of what God should be like. Grace leads a person to

---

[100] Ephesians 2:8-9 (NIV). See also Titus 2:11.
[101] 2 Corinthians 12:9.
[102] Hebrews 13:9.
[103] 1 Corinthians 15:10.
[104] See Matthew 5:45.
[105] See Proverbs 29:13.
[106] See Acts 14:16-17.
[107] Psalm 145:9 and Luke 6:35.
[108] Genesis 1:27.
[109] Philip Yancey, *What's So Amazing About Grace?* Grand Rapids, Michigan: Zondervan Publishing House, 1997.

forgive others despite unspeakable crimes.[110] It leads one person to keep forgiving another for repeating the same offense countless times.[111] It leads us to love our enemies, to pray for them, and do good to them.[112] And above all, it's what led God to send his Son to earth in human form to live a sinless life filled with suffering and persecution, and die horribly and unjustly at our hands so that we might have eternal life.[113]

The last statement is pretty amazing. The Bible describes a God who loves us so deeply that, even though we repeatedly choose to turn our backs on him, He would sacrifice His only Son to have a relationship with us. I don't know of any faith that describes such a personal God, one who reaches down to mankind rather than requiring us to reach up via our own efforts—a God who endures deep humiliation in order to save us.

The Bible is a love story, one describing a father's (God's) incredible love for his children (His creation), and it's filled with examples of God's grace toward us—all of us. Throughout history, God has expressed His love for people who would be considered scoundrels by society and used them in His service. God took an adulterer and murderer (King David) and molded him into someone whom many consider to be the greatest king in Old Testament times. He also took a murderer and torturer (the apostle Paul) and changed him into the greatest missionary of all time. Paul himself wrote:

> *Christ Jesus came into the world to save sinners—and I am the worst of them all. But God had mercy on me so that Christ Jesus could use me as a prime example of his great patience with even the worst sinners. Then others will realize that they, too, can believe in him and receive eternal life.*[114]

---

[110] See Acts 7:60.
[111] See Matthew 18:22.
[112] See Matthew 5:44-47 and Luke 6:27-31.
[113] See John 3:16 and Philippians 2:5-8.
[114] 1 Timothy 1:15-16.

Jesus was all about grace. He had a reputation for hanging out with people society judged as sinners and outcasts: lepers, prostitutes, foreigners, and tax collectors. He told grace stories like the one describing a father's outrageous love and forgiveness for his son who took an early withdrawal of his inheritance and blew it on partying and prostitutes.[115] He acted gracefully, like when he deftly prevented a mob from stoning a woman caught in adultery.[116] And He talked about how a celebration breaks out in heaven whenever a single sinner repents.[117]

While I saw and was moved by examples of grace in the world and the Bible over the years, I didn't come to understand its realness, power, impact, or beauty until I experienced it on a deep, personal level through my divorce.

<u>The Gospel in God's Words</u>

The word "Gospel" appears 101 times across ninety-five verses in the King James version of the New Testament. It appears in both noun form, where it means "good news," and verb form where it means "to bring good news." This good news is that, while we are *all* sinners and subject to God's judgement, we can be reconciled to God through Jesus' sacrifice, adopted into God's family, and given all the rights that come along with being His sons and daughters. Consider the following scriptures:

- 1 Corinthians 15:1-4: *Let me now remind you, dear brothers and sisters, of the Good News I preached to you before... It is this Good News that saves you if you continue to believe the message I told you...I passed on to you what was most important and what had also been*

[115] Luke 15:11-32.
[116] John 8:1-11.
[117] Luke 15:3-7.

passed on to me. Christ died for our sins, just as the Scriptures said. He was buried, and he was raised from the dead on the third day, just as the Scriptures said.

- Romans 1:16-17: *For I am not ashamed of this Good News about Christ. It is the power of God at work, saving everyone who believes—the Jew first and also the Gentile. This Good News tells us how God makes us right in his sight. This is accomplished from start to finish by faith.*

So, belief in the sacrifice of Jesus Christ for our sins, and his resurrection, has the power to make us right in God's sight and save us. But why do we need to be saved, and from what do we need to be saved? Here are more scriptures to consider:

- Romans 3:23: *For everyone has sinned; we all fall short of God's glorious standard.*
- James 2:10: *For the person who keeps all the laws except one is as guilty as a person who has broken all of God's laws.*
- Romans 6:23: *For the wages of sin is death, but the free gift of God is eternal life through Christ Jesus our Lord.*
- John 3:16 (NIV): *For God so loved the world that he gave his one and only Son, that whoever believes in him shall not perish but have eternal life.*
- Ephesians 2:8-9: *God saved you by his grace when you believed [in Christ's sacrifice and resurrection]. And you can't take credit for this; it is a gift from God. Salvation is not a reward for the good things we have done, so none of us can boast about it.*
- Acts 20:20-21: *I [Paul] never shrank back from telling you what you needed to hear, either publicly or in your homes. I have had one message for Jews and Greeks*

alike—the necessity of repenting from sin and turning to God, and of having faith in our Lord Jesus.

- Acts 4:8,12: *Then Peter, filled with the Holy Spirit, said... There is salvation in no one else [other than Jesus Christ]! God has given no other name under heaven by which we must be saved.*
- Roman 10:9: *If you confess with your mouth that Jesus is Lord and believe in your heart that God raised him from the dead, you will be saved. For it is by believing in your heart that you are made right with God, and it is by openly declaring your faith that you are saved.*
- Romans 5:8 (NIV): *But God demonstrates his own love for us in this: While we were still sinners, Christ died for us.*

In short, we are all sinners and under a death penalty. God sent Christ to die in our place, and if we recognize our sinfulness, repent of it, and accept Jesus' sacrifice and resurrection, we are given eternal life that is free from sin, pain, suffering, war, and tears.

Some theologians have said that the Gospel is almost-too-good-to-be-true news given how fantastic it is. Even though we do nothing to deserve it and there is no way we can earn it, God is willing to forgive and forget all our sins if we simply accept what Jesus has done for us.[118]

Passion and boldness

In 2009, the American rock band Rage Against the Machine was part of a campaign to top the United Kingdom's music singles sales chart during Christmas week. If successful, they would join something known as the Christmas Number Ones list. They offered to perform a free concert in Finsbury Park if their fans downloaded

[118] Romans 3:23-28, 4:4-8, and 5:12-21.

enough copies of their song "Killing in the Name" to propel them to the top of the charts. It was an act of defiance against what band members described as the "sterile pop monopoly" in the U.K.[119]

In the end, the band sold 500,000 downloaded copies of its song, handily beating its main competitor. The concert was on. I happened to stumble across a broadcast of the show while channel surfing one night and was astonished at what I saw. Thousands of fans were jammed into the outdoor venue and their response to the band was surreal. At times the crowd looked like a great swelling wave of humanity as people jumped in unison to the music. The level of passion expressed by the fans for the band was remarkable.

In September 2018, I went to a prayer event on the National Mall in Washington, D.C. It was the fourth such event in five years that was organized by a group that has encouraged hundreds of churches in the D.C. Metro Area to commit to removing the divides that separate them and to saturate the D.C. area with the Gospel. Since the first two events were attended by five and seven thousand people, respectively, I was expecting a significant crowd. What I saw was disappointing. There couldn't have been more than 150 people there in addition to the volunteers, speakers, and performers.

I heard lots of reasons for why people didn't show up. It was cloudy with a chance of rain. It was on a Saturday and people were with their families. Parents needed to take their children to sporting events, etc. *What the heck has happened to us?!* I thought. How can we be so passionate about a band or sports teams or companies like Apple and have so little passion for God and His amazing message of grace? There have been better-attended Christian events for sure, and I'm not advocating the hysteria displayed at the Rage Against the Machine concert, but when it came time to sacrifice *one* morning to gather together, pray, and magnify God's message of hope, we blew it.

---

[119] *Rage Against the Machine beat X Factor winner in charts*, BBC News, December 20, 2009. See: http://news.bbc.co.uk/2/hi/entertainment/8423340.stm.

Our passion for God in America is weak and getting weaker by the day. We'll fight like mad to elect judges to implement laws that most people won't honor, but we won't take the time to humble ourselves before God, petition Him, and trust that He will answer by changing people's hearts.

I went to the prayer event because I have learned about the realness, power, and impact of God's grace through my experiences with Diane, and I cannot stop sharing the wonderful things I have experienced.

All Christians have the "incredible greatness of God's power" at work in their lives,[120] and "through [this] mighty power at work within us, [God can] accomplish infinitely more than we might ask or think."[121] Do we really believe this? I do. I've experienced it. And anyone else can, too.

We have this power at our disposal, but it starts with the hard and unglamorous work of humbling ourselves before God and our neighbors, praying without ceasing, delving into and trusting God's Word, and expressing the radical love of Jesus Christ to *everyone*. I think this is what Jesus meant when He said we must take up our crosses daily.[122] Only then will we be unstoppable in passionately and boldly sharing God's Gospel of grace with everyone we meet.

A little over a year ago, a well-known, local, Christian tech executive told me that I was "completely overboard" with my faith and that people aren't interested in the story of my relationship with Diane. I walked away from our lunch a bit rattled and wondered if what he said was true. I shared his comments with two mature Christian friends, and they both laughed. They said that was proof that I'm doing exactly what I'm supposed to be doing.

I hope and pray that this executive is wrong, and that countless people choose to let Jesus express His radical grace through them. I hope they freely share their excitement about God's Word and aren't

---

[120] Ephesians 1:19-20.
[121] Ephesians 3:20.
[122] Luke 9:23.

afraid to say the names *Jesus* or *God* in front of anyone. It's the only hope we have to see genuine change in our nation and around the world.

19 | Monumental Hug

About sixteen months before Diane passed away, my pastor preached a sermon about the importance of creating monuments to the most significant moments in our lives. He had the ushers hand out small stones and markers and asked each of us to write a word on our stone that captured one of those moments.

It occurred to me that Diane's thankful hug as I left her new apartment the day after she had moved out of our home was the greatest turning point of my life. It was a monumental hug, so to speak, so I wrote "hug" on the stone and placed it on my work desk as a reminder.

As I considered various titles for this book, the term "monumental hug" stood out as the obvious choice. I also made numerous attempts at including a photo of the stone on the cover but ran into various problems.

Then I came across a photo of Diane and me hugging that Shannon had taken without our knowledge. I was helping Diane move from her bed to the bathroom one evening during the final week of her life. After slowly walking the length and width of her bed, Diane sat on the bottom corner of the bed to rest. When she rose a few minutes later, she decided to give me a hug. Shannon took the picture looking through the doorway to Diane's bedroom. I soon concluded that her picture is the perfect match to the book's title.

I'm banking on the hug Diane gave me the day she moved into her own apartment and the one she gave me just before she passed away to be monuments to the power of God's grace to radically change our lives. Your life.

Appendix A | The Toll of Cancer

What follows are some data points on the physical, financial, and emotional toll that Diane's illness took on her and those around her. While it's a hard and raw way of looking at things, it's also worth reviewing.

21 months	The number of months Diane lived following the discovery of a tumor in her pancreas
17 months	The number of consecutive months that Diane received chemotherapy treatments
14 months	The number of months that Diane lived beyond the prediction that she would more than likely not live past February 2017
39 treatments	The total number of chemotherapy treatments Diane received: 5 Folfirinox and 34 Gemzar/Abraxane
$486,957.00	The total amount Diane's oncology practice charged her health insurance company for chemotherapy treatments. The actual amount reimbursed is unclear
$73,475.00	The total amount the oncologist billed Diane's health insurance company for five Neulasta shots that accompanied the Folfirinox treatments

$31,865.70	The amount of money Diane spent in 2017 on health insurance coverage, her maximum out-of-pocket costs, and alternative treatments including supplements, CBD oil, acupuncture, chiropractic care, etc.
$108,000	Base income Diane lost because she could not work while undergoing chemotherapy treatments and wrestling with the myriad of physical, emotional, financial, and administrative issues associated with her illness
20 months	The number of months of work Diane missed while fighting her illness
3 months	The period of time that Diane experienced significant physical pain due to the spread of her cancer
4 weeks	The period of time that Diane ate very-little-to-nothing at the end of her life
4 weeks	The period of time that Diane went without a bowel movement at the end of her life
2 weeks	The period of time that Diane struggled with vomiting at the end of her life
9 days	The maximum number of days that Diane could not leave her apartment in 2016 due to unpredictable diarrhea brought about by chemotherapy

36 hours	The amount of time that Diane was minimally responsive at the end of her life
18 seconds	The greatest length of time measured between Diane's breaths while she slept in the last month of her life. Amazingly, this was *not* in her last week
123 pounds	Diane's peak weight in the later part of 2017
103 pounds	Diane's weight at the beginning of April 2018
80-to-90 pounds	Diane's estimated weight at the end of her life
854 pills	The number of supplement pills Diane took every four weeks to build up her immune system while on her second chemo regimen (Gemzar/Abraxane). This does not include numerous powders, liquids, and CBD oil that she also consumed
107 days	The number of days Diane visited her oncologist's office for doctor appointments, chemotherapy, blood work, and nurse visits. This does *not* include surgeon visits, emergency room visits, outpatient procedures, acupuncture visits, trips to other states, meetings with a cancer counselor, etc.

Appendix B | If You're Diagnosed with Cancer

What follows is my grossly simple, yet hopefully helpful, outline of what I think any person should do if diagnosed with cancer (or any other life-threatening illness). Please think and pray about it.

- Before you do anything, STOP and take a deep breath. There is no need to rush a care decision in most cases.
- Decide to attack things at all three levels of your being, i.e., in your spirit, soul, and physical body.
- Seek God's wisdom and direction with humility, thanksgiving, praise and repentance.
- Place God at the center of everything you do regarding your treatment. Persistently seek God's guidance, pray, get in His Word, seek support in community, be hopeful, and practice forgiveness.
- Find and visit a local Christian healing ministry.
- Trust that your life will bring honor to Christ whether you live or die.
- Take sufficient time to make your treatment decisions at different stages.
- Get second opinions from people you know are trustworthy.
- Once made, believe in your treatment decision and walk boldly and joyfully.
- Get molecular testing done *before* choosing a chemo treatment and use it to guide your decision.
- Strongly consider trying a non-toxic treatment approach before going the chemo route. Many harmful effects of chemo cannot be undone.

- Seek high quality alternative treatment resources. If you chose an alternative approach, don't do a little here and a little there. Go all in.
- Remember that this is a journey. Grace is patient with those around us as they walk their journey. If someone you love is doing something differently than what you think he or she should do, or moving more slowly than you think appropriate, pray for God to give you the wisdom and ability to support your loved one no matter what and to offer advice as gracefully as possible.

(11/6/19)

Made in the USA
Lexington, KY
20 December 2019

58791551R00107